Activity Workbook

ExpressWays

Second Edition

3

Steven J. Molinsky

Bill Bliss

Contributing Author

Dorothy Lynde

D1300850

Longman

Publisher: *Louisa B. Hellegers*
Electronic Production Editor: *Carey Davies*
Manufacturing Manager: *Ray Keating*

Electronic Art Production Supervision: *Todd Ware*
Electronic Art Production/Scanning: *Marita Froimson*
Art Director: *Merle Krumper*
Interior Design: *Ken Liao*

Illustrator: *Richard Hill*

The authors gratefully acknowledge the contribution of Tina Carver in the development of the *ExpressWays* program.

© 1997 by PRENTICE HALL REGENTS
A Pearson Education Company
Pearson Education
10 Bank Street
White Plains, NY 10606

All rights reserved. No part of this book may be reproduced, in any form or by any means, without permission in writing from the publisher.
Printed in the United States of America

20 19 18 17 16 15 14 13 12 11

ISBN 0-13-570896-6

EXPRESSWAYS 3 Activity Workbook TRAVEL GUIDE

Exit 1 • Meeting and Greeting People Giving Information

Greet Someone and Introduce Yourself 1

Introduce Members of Your Family 4

Give Information About Countries and Nationalities 5

Provide Information When Checking In to a Hotel 7

Exchange Information 9

Exit 2 • Sharing News and Information

Tell About Past Events 13

Talk with Friends, Neighbors, and Co-Workers 16

Tell About Weekend Plans 19

Tell About Yourself and Your Family 22

Exit 3 • People and Places

Call Directory Assistance 25

Make Telephone Calls 27

Access Public Transportation 29

Give Directions to Places in the Community 31

Give Directions for Traveling by Car 34

CHECK-UP TEST: Exits 1, 2, 3 37

Exit 4 • Housing and Food

Describe Features of an Apartment 39

Enumerate Food Items 41

Locate Items in a Supermarket 43

Evaluate the Cost of Food Items 45

Discuss Ingredients 47

Give Recipe Instructions 49

Exit 5 • At Work

Tell About Work Skills 51

Tell About Work-Related Events 52

Tell About Accomplishments and Experiences 54

Express Confidence About Your Abilities 56

Discuss Job Performance 57

Tell About Work Experience 58

Tell About Job Responsibilities 60

Analyze Successful Job Interview Strategies 61

Exit 6 • Health and Emergencies

Report an Emergency 63

Report an Accident 64

Ask for Recommendations in a Drug Store 65

Describe Symptoms and Make a Doctor's Appointment 66

Ask About and Give a Medical History 68

Receive a Doctor's Medical Advice 70

Receive a Pharmacist's Directions 71

Offer Someone Medical Advice 73

CHECK-UP TEST: Exits 4, 5, 6 74

Exit 7 • Shopping

Locate Items in a Department Store 76

Select Items in a Department Store 78

Purchase Items in a Department Store 80

Return Items to a Department Store 82

Access the Services of a Post Office 84

Discuss Features of Products 86

Exit 8 • Recreation

Make Plans 87

Discuss Recreation Preferences 88

Extend Invitations 90

Decline Invitations 91

Tell About Weekend Activities 93

Tell About Experiences 95

Use the Newspaper to Make Movie Plans 96

Discuss Television Preferences 98

CHECK-UP TEST: Exits 7, 8 99

APPENDIX

Scripts for Listening Exercises 101

Correlation: *ExpressWays Student Text/Activity Workbook* 106

Exit 1

Greet Someone and Introduce Yourself

Student Text Pages 2–7

A. The Right Choice

Circle the correct words.

A. You're new here, (aren't you / you aren't) [1] ?

B. Yes, I (do / am) [2] . My name is Ken Watson.

A. (I name / I'm) [3] Sue Potter. Nice to meet you.

B. (Nice meeting you, too / Nice to meeting you, too) [4] .

A. Tell me, which department (are you working / do you work in) [5] ?

B. Shipping. (What are you / What about you) [6] ?

A. Accounting.

B. Listen

Listen and circle the word you hear.

1	(Which)	What	3	What	Whose	5	Who	Whose
2	Whose	Who	4	How	Who	6	Why	What

C. Wrong Way!

Put the lines in the correct order.

___ Hello. I'm Rosa Gomez. Nice to meet you.

_1_ Hello. Let me introduce myself. I'm your neighbor. My name is Barry Burns.

___ Nice meeting you, too. Tell me, what floor do you live on?

___ The 4th.

___ The 9th. And you?

D. What's the Response?

Choose the correct response.

1. Where are you from?
   a. English.
   (b.) England.

2. Who is your neighbor?
   a. I don't know.
   b. I'm a good neighbor.

3. When did you move in?
   a. Next Tuesday.
   b. Yesterday.

4. I'm enjoying my new job. How about you?
   a. I have some good days and some bad days.
   b. You do.

5. Whose class are you in?
   a. Spanish.
   b. Mr. Cramer's.

6. How are you enjoying your new neighbors?
   a. On Mondays for dinner.
   b. They're very nice.

7. Why are you here?
   a. I came to study accounting.
   b. I moved in two weeks ago.

8. What floor do you live on?
   a. 8B.
   b. The 8th.

9. Which department do you work in?
   a. The 7th.
   b. Personnel.

10. Tell me, how are you enjoying your classes?
    a. Oh, they have their ups and downs.
    b. Accounting and History.

11. Which apartment do you live in?
    a. 6D.
    b. It's small.

12. I'm a mechanic at Al's Garage. How about you?
    a. How do you do?
    b. I work at the library.

E. The Right Choice

Circle the correct word.

1. A. When (do (did)) you move in?
   B. Two weeks ago.
2. A. (Do Am) I going to be okay, Dr. DiMarco?
   B. You're going to be fine.
3. A. When (do are) you start classes?
   B. Next week.
4. A. How (is are) you enjoying school?
   B. I like it a lot.
5. A. (Is Does) your son have a car?
   B. No. He has a motorcycle.
6. A. When (is do) the new tenant going to move in?
   B. I'm not sure.
7. A. (Do Are) you sure?
   B. I'm positive!
8. A. (Do Is) your teachers give a lot of homework?
   B. Yes. We have homework every day.

F. Listen

Listen and decide what they're talking about.

1	(transportation)	housing	4	health	housing	7	health	school
2	housing	work	5	work	housing	8	transportation	work
3	work	school	6	health	work	9	housing	work

G. WordRap: *Meeting People*

Listen. Then clap and practice.

A. You live here, don't you?
B. Yes, I do.
A. What's your name?
B. My name is Sue.

A. You're new here, aren't you?
B. Yes, I am.
A. What's your name?
B. My name is Sam.

A. You teach here, don't you?
B. Yes, I do.
A. Where's your class?
B. In Room 202.

A. You study here, don't you?
B. Yes, I do.
A. Who's your teacher?
B. Mr. Crew.

Introduce Members of Your Family

Student Text
Pages 8–9

A. More Formal or Less Formal?

Decide whether the following are "more formal" or "less formal."

	More Formal	*Less Formal*
1 "How do you do?"	✓	
2 "How are you doing?"		
3 "I'd like you to meet my husband, Vincent."		
4 "This is my son, Billy."		
5 "How are things?"		
6 "Let me introduce you to my father, Mr. Sanchez."		
7 "I'd like to introduce my mother-in-law, Mrs. Ames."		
8 "Hi."		

B. Listen

Listen and choose the correct people.

1 ✓ ___

2 ___ ___

3 ___ ___

4 ___ ___

5 ___ ___

6 ___ ___

C. Wrong Way!

Put the words in the correct order.

1 doing? are How you
How are you doing?

2 things? How are
_____

3 my I'd Jane. to introduce wife, like
_____

4 you. meeting It's nice
_____

Give Information About Countries and Nationalities

Student Text Pages 10–11

A. Wrong Way!

Put the lines in the correct order.

1

___ Colombian?

___ Where in Colombia are you from?

_1_ Passport, please!

___ I'm not surprised. A lot of Colombians are on vacation at this time of year.

___ Yes.

___ Bogotá.

___ Here you are.

___ There sure are a lot of people from Colombia visiting right now.

2

_1_ How long do you plan to stay?

___ Thank you.

___ Next!

___ All right. Here's your passport. Welcome to the United States.

___ About three weeks.

B. Matching Lines

Match the lines.

_e_	**1** Are you Australian?	a. Florence.
___	**2** What's your favorite food?	b. I don't know yet.
___	**3** Do you speak Vietnamese?	c. Is Kyoto in Japan?
___	**4** What's your favorite Canadian city?	d. Yes. I'm from Rio de Janeiro.
___	**5** I'm going to travel to Kyoto soon.	e. No. I'm South African.
___	**6** Is Seoul a city in China?	f. No. It's in Korea.
___	**7** Where in Italy are you from?	g. Sushi.
___	**8** Are you Brazilian?	h. Montreal.
___	**9** Where are you going on vacation?	i. Just a little.

C. Crosswalk

ACROSS

3. _____ is in France.
5. _____ is the capital of Japan.
7. _____ is my favorite city in Italy.
8. Remember to visit _____ when you go to Spain.

DOWN

1. _____ is a city in Brazil.
2. _____ is my favorite city in Canada.
4. _____ is the capital of Sweden.
6. _____ is in Korea.

D. Listen

Listen and circle the correct word.

1	(Italian)	Italy	4	Spaniard	Spanish	7	French	France
2	Japan	Japanese	5	Brazilian	Brazil	8	Spanish	Colombian
3	Swedes	Swedish	6	Korean	Korea	9	Canadian	French

E. Open Road!

Tell about yourself.

1. What's your favorite country to visit? .....
2. Why do you like to go there? .....
3. What languages do you speak? .....
4. Where did you go on your last vacation? .....
5. Where are you going on your next vacation? .....

Provide Information When Checking In to a Hotel

Student Text Pages 12–13

A. The Right Choice

Circle the correct words.

A. May I help you?

B. Yes. I have a [respiration / (reservation)] [1].

A. [Whose / What's] [2] your last name?

B. Spencer.

A. Could you [say / spell] [3] that, please?

B. S–P–E–N–C–E–R.

A. [First / Front] [4] name Veronica?

B. That's [collect / correct] [5].

A. I see here you [requested / connected] [6] twin beds.

B. [Not ready / Not really] [7]. I requested a king-size bed.

A. Oh. I guess we had the wrong information in the computer. [No people / No problem] [8].

B. What's the Word?

Complete the sentences.

reservation	facing	suite	alone	bed	charging	staying	check in

1. My name is Harold Baines, and I have a reservation.
2. According to our records, you requested a _____.
3. I'll be _____ for two nights.
4. Are you _____ your bill to American Express?
5. I requested a king-size _____.
6. Are you traveling _____ or with your family?
7. I asked for a room _____ the park.
8. You need to _____ at the front desk.

C. Listen

Listen and choose the correct response.

1. (a.) Yes. I have a reservation.
   b. Yes. I'll help you.
2. a. That's correct.
   b. Not really.
3. a. I'm traveling by bus.
   b. I'm traveling with my family.
4. a. Yes. I'm checking in.
   b. No. I'm charging my bill.
5. a. No. I requested a reservation.
   b. No, actually not. I requested a suite.
6. a. Three days.
   b. I'm staying with my family.
7. a. That's right.
   b. I asked for a check facing the park.
8. a. Could you spell that, please?
   b. And your last name?

D. Open Road!

This hotel has the wrong information about your reservation. Complete the conversation any way you wish.

A. I'm sorry, but we don't have your request for a suite in our computer.

B. .....

A. .....

B. .....

A. .....

B. .....

Exchange Information

Student Text
Pages 14–17

A. Open Road!

You hurt yourself! What do you say at the hospital?

A. Before the doctor sees you, we need some information. What's your last name?

B. .....

A. Could you spell that, please?

B. .....

A. And your first name?

B .....

A. Address?

B. .....

A. Telephone number?

B. .....

A. What's your date of birth?

B. .....

A. And what's your Social Security number?

B. .....

A. Do you have medical insurance?

B. .....

A. Do you know the I.D. number?

B. .....

A. Take a seat over there, and somebody will see you in a few minutes.

B. What's the Question?

Complete the conversations.

1. What's your apartment number ?
   4C.

2. _____?
   (902) 559-2375.

3. _____?
   02246.

4. _____?
   12/4/72.

C. What Are They Saying?

What are these people expressing?

1. This person is ____.
   a. greeting someone
   b. asking for information

2. This person is ____.
   a. asking for information
   b. introducing someone

3. This person is ____.
   a. correcting someone
   b. greeting someone

4. This person is ____.
   a. asking for information
   b. giving information

5. This person is ____.
   a. introducing someone
   b. greeting someone

6. This person is ____.
   a. greeting someone
   b. asking for information

D. Analogies

student	Not really.	university	work	telephone number
came	Biology	difficult	This is Tom.	in a little while

1. How do you do? : Hi! *as* Let me introduce you to Tom. : This is Tom.
2. live : apartment *as* study : _____
3. supervisor : worker *as* teacher : _____
4. have : had *as* come : _____
5. late : early *as* easy : _____
6. move in : apartment *as* major in : _____
7. yes : That's correct. *as* no : _____
8. zip code : address *as* area code : _____
9. why : because it snowed *as* when : _____
10. passport number : travel *as* Social Security number : _____

E. Word Search

Find the names of 10 family members.

R	I	P	D	G	S	L	O	U	T	L	S	I	F	Z	B	B	O	P
D	L	E	B	A	I	J	Y	L	X	H	W	P	L	L	A	W	A	Y
A	O	K	E	Q	S	A	C	T	P	H	R	A	W	L	N	C	M	M
U	E	R	P	U	T	S	O	N	G	S	L	Q	O	D	G	K	U	O
G	T	C	S	E	A	N	A	F	A	T	H	U	P	B	U	O	U	T
H	E	P	H	E	K	U	P	A	N	N	S	N	P	R	N	P	K	H
T	L	O	P	X	E	P	T	A	I	O	P	E	P	O	P	L	Z	E
E	Y	W	R	Y	O	P	G	H	E	P	S	P	H	T	Z	C	B	R
R	Q	E	T	U	U	P	A	A	C	S	C	H	T	H	O	W	N	P
W	I	V	E	T	M	A	F	A	E	H	I	E	F	E	W	I	F	E
H	B	R	O	T	H	E	R	S	D	A	H	W	A	G	N	E	I	C
M	O	T	H	E	E	R	W	O	D	A	U	G	H	T	S	U	N	N
N	S	I	S	T	E	R	C	O	E	Y	S	B	R	T	T	T	A	U
A	D	G	J	K	R	L	X	N	N	W	B	T	U	O	S	P	A	G
N	K	L	D	S	O	Y	N	G	L	X	A	W	Y	O	N	C	P	C
U	C	L	A	L	K	E	M	U	T	D	N	W	P	A	W	A	E	J
P	U	T	F	A	T	H	E	R	S	V	D	W	R	D	E	W	P	P

F. Matching Lines

Match the situations.

h	1 "Hi."	a. Asking about a course
___	2 "How do you do?"	b. Asking about a boss
___	3 "When did you move in?"	c. Checking in at a hotel
___	4 "What days does it meet?"	d. Meeting in a formal situation
___	5 "Do you have medical insurance?"	e. Asking about a teacher
___	6 "Which department do you work in?"	f. Talking to a new neighbor
___	7 "Do you have a reservation?"	g. Going through customs
___	8 "Does he give a lot of tests?"	h. Meeting in an informal situation
___	9 "Who is your supervisor?"	i. Meeting someone at work
___	10 "How long do you plan to stay in this country?"	j. Giving information at the hospital

G. Open Road!

Complete the following any way you wish and then compare with a classmate.

1. What questions do you ask a new neighbor?

.....

.....

.....

2. What questions do you ask a new co-worker?

.....

.....

.....

3. What questions do they ask when you register for a course?

.....

.....

.....

4. What questions do they ask when you go through customs?

.....

.....

.....

5. What does the hotel clerk ask when you register at a hotel?

.....

.....

.....

6. What do they ask when you go to the hospital emergency room?

.....

.....

.....

Exit 2

Tell About Past Events

Student Text Pages 20–23

A. What's the Response?

Choose the correct response.

1. I just got a big promotion.
   (a.) Congratulations!
   b. I'm so sorry.

2. You seem upset. Is anything wrong?
   a. Yes, it's wrong.
   b. Yes, there is.

3. I have some bad news.
   a. Did you break up with Alice?
   b. Did you win the lottery?

4. That's fantastic!
   a. I think so, too.
   b. How about you?

5. I didn't receive any birthday presents.
   a. Is anything wrong?
   b. I'm very sorry to hear that.

6. All my plants died while I was away!
   a. What a shame!
   b. Why a shame!

7. What's new with you?
   a. How about you?
   b. Nothing much.

8. I didn't get the raise I was hoping for.
   a. That's a shame!
   b. That's great!

9. What's happening with you?
   a. I'm happening.
   b. Nothing much.

10. I have some good news.
    a. Did you pass your driver's test?
    b. Did you fail your driver's test?

11. I don't feel very well today.
    a. That's too bad!
    b. That's wonderful!

12. What's wrong?
    a. I have some good news.
    b. I have some bad news.

B. Listen

Listen and decide if it's "good news" or "bad news."

1	Good News	(Bad News)	6	Good News	Bad News
2	Good News	Bad News	7	Good News	Bad News
3	Good News	Bad News	8	Good News	Bad News
4	Good News	Bad News	9	Good News	Bad News
5	Good News	Bad News	10	Good News	Bad News

C. The Right Choice

Circle the correct word.

1. My husband (make (made)) me a cake for my birthday this year.
2. My friends (left leave) work early today. I wonder why!
3. My mother-in-law (take took) a plane to Miami last week.
4. I'm really hungry! I (ate didn't eat) breakfast this morning.
5. Last month I (went go) to Brazil on vacation. It was great!
6. Do you remember Bob Bennett? I (see saw) him yesterday.
7. Joe didn't go to work today. He (felt didn't feel) well.
8. I (got get) my husband a tie for his birthday this year.
9. I have some bad news! I (didn't win won) the lottery yesterday.
10. I looked for my keys in the office, but I (found didn't find) them.
11. I have some good news. I finally (didn't get got) a job yesterday!
12. I'm sorry you (didn't buy bought) that blue sweater. It was beautiful!
13. I (wrote write) to my parents last week to tell them about my new apartment.
14. Susie forgot her homework yesterday. I (have to had to) take it to her at school.

D. WordRap: *Bad News!*

Listen. Then clap and practice.

A. What happened to Tad?
He looks so sad.
B. He lost his job.
A. That's too bad!

A. What's wrong with Mame?
She looks the same.
B. Her goldfish died.
A. What a shame!

A. What's wrong with Dad?
He looks so mad.
B. His car was stolen.
A. That's too bad!

A. What's wrong with Sue?
She looks so blue.
B. Her rent went up.
A. Mine did, too.

E. Greeting Card Match

Match the cards.

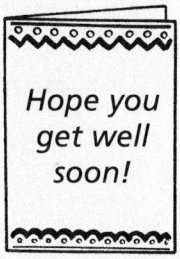

1 c 2 ___ 3 ___ 4 ___

5 ___ 6 ___ 7 ___ 8 ___

F. Open Road!

Write your own greeting for a special occasion.

.....

.....

.....

Talk with Friends, Neighbors, and Co-workers

Student Text Pages 24–27

A. The Right Choice

Circle the correct word.

A. Henry?

B. Yes?

A. Can I [1] asked / (ask) you a question?

B. Sure. [2] What / Why ?

A. [3] Do / Did the boss [4] fire / fired his secretary this morning?

B. No. The boss didn't [5] fires / fire his secretary. Where [6] do / did you [7] hear / heard that?

A. I [8] hear / heard it in the cafeteria.

B. Well, I can't [9] believed / believe it's true. I'm sure [10] its / it's just a rumor.

B. Open Road!

Tell about a rumor you heard.

C. Listen

Listen and write the number under the correct picture.

___

___

___

1

___

___

___

___

D. The Right Choice

Circle the correct word.

1. Can I (tell (ask)) you a question?
2. Our supervisor (wents wants) to shorten our coffee break.
3. Someone mentioned it at the bus (driver stop).
4. I think the (boss loss) is going to fire me.
5. The taxi drivers plan to go on (fight strike) at midnight.
6. I can't believe it's (true false). I'm sure it's just a rumor.
7. The (apartment people) across the hall are getting a divorce.
8. (When Who) did you hear that?
9. He (heard beard) it at the office.
10. Our gym teacher (saw was) in the Olympics.
11. The whole school is (talking waking) about it!
12. (When Who) told you that?
13. I (told overheard) some people talking about it.
14. Our English teacher is going to (hit quit).
15. I didn't (receive believe) any birthday cards this year!
16. They were talking about it at our (union onion) meeting.

E. What's the Line?

Complete the conversations.

1. A. I hear the Apex Corporation wants to buy our company.
   B. No. They ___don't want___ to buy OUR company. They _____ to buy the company across the street.

2. A. Is our supervisor going to quit?
   B. No. Our supervisor _____ to quit. I think it's just a rumor.

3. A. I hear that Roger is getting a divorce.
   B. That's not true. He _____ a divorce. _____ married!

4. A. Does the boss plan to lay off the managers?
   B. No. She _____ to lay off the managers. But I think she _____ to lay off some of the secretaries.

5. A. Are the workers going to have to take a pay cut?
   B. No. They _____ to have to take a pay cut. Where did you hear that?

6. A. I hear that Melissa wants to leave the company.
   B. That's not true. She _____ to leave the company. She _____ to take a vacation.

7. A. Is it true that sales were bad this month?
   B. Where did you hear that? Sales _____ bad this month. In fact, they _____ very good!

F. Yes or No?

Is it a rumor? Check Yes or No.

		Yes	*No*
1	"The teachers are going on strike. I heard it on the radio."	___	✓
2	"The boss is planning to lay us off. I heard it in the cafeteria."	✓	___
3	"I overheard in the elevator that we're all getting raises."	___	___
4	"Ten airline pilots just quit. I heard it on the 6 o'clock news."	___	___
5	"Mrs. Fleming was in the Olympics. I saw her gold medal."	___	___
6	"Someone told me the bookkeeper won the lottery yesterday."	___	___
7	"A few people mentioned that we might have to take a cut in pay."	___	___
8	"The mayor wrecked his car last night. I read it in the paper."	___	___
9	"Mike told me that one of the supervisors thinks they're planning to close the factory."	___	___

Tell About Weekend Plans

Student Text
Pages 28–29

A. The Right Choice

Circle the correct words.

A. What are you going / go [1] to do this weekend?

B. My wife and I am going / are going [2] to have a birthday party for our daughter.

A. A birthday party for your daughter?! We're / You're [3] certainly going / go [4] to be busy!

B. I suppose so. Now / How [5] about you? What is / are [6] YOUR plans for the weekend?

A. I don't know for sure. I'm pretty sure I'll be going / go [7] to the beach.

B. Well, have / do [8] a good weekend!

A. You, too / do [9].

B. Open Road!

Tell about YOUR weekend plans.

.....

.....

.....

C. What's the Question?

Complete the questions.

When	Where	What	How many	Why	Who

1. A. ___Where___ are you going to plant those flowers?
   B. I'm going to plant them in my garden.
2. A. _____ are you going to repaint your bedroom?
   B. I'm going to repaint it this summer.
3. A. _____ are you going to do this weekend?
   B. I'm going to finish my term paper.
4. A. _____ friends are coming to your party?
   B. About 20 friends are coming.
5. A. _____ will you put these old photos?
   B. I'll put them in the attic.
6. A. _____ will tell the family the good news?
   B. Dad will tell everyone this weekend.
7. A. _____ are they going to lay off the workers?
   B. Because business isn't very good.
8. A. _____ is your daughter going to do when she finishes school?
   B. She's going to look for a job as an accountant.
9. A. _____ will you tell your parents you're getting married?
   B. I think I'll tell them this weekend.

D. Function Check

What are these people expressing?

1	"I'm going to see a movie."	(a.) certainty	b. uncertainty
2	"I'm not positive."	a. certainty	b. uncertainty
3	"I'll probably clean my house."	a. probability	b. improbability
4	"I'll most likely see a movie."	a. probability	b. improbability
5	"I'm pretty sure I'll come."	a. probability	b. improbability
6	"I don't know for sure."	a. certainty	b. uncertainty
7	"I'll be there at three o'clock."	a. certainty	b. uncertainty
8	"I promise I'll finish the report today."	a. certainty	b. probability

E. Listen

Listen and number the activities.

1 3 1 2 2 _____ _____ _____

3 _____ _____ _____ 4 _____ _____ _____

F. Crosswalk

ACROSS

2 Many people do _____ at home on the weekend.

4 You end a marriage when you get a _____.

5 A good place to go when it's hot is the _____.

7 When you paint a second time, you _____.

DOWN

1 People plant flowers in a _____.

2 Children love to go to the _____.

3 You can ask your boss for a _____.

6 Before people get married, they get _____.

7 I heard a _____ at work. I don't think it's true.

8 I'm going to a birthday _____.

Tell About Yourself and Your Family

Student Text
Pages 30–33

A. Wrong Way!

Put the lines in the correct order.

1. ___ Gee . . . uh. I don't know where to begin. What do you want to know?
   ___ No, I'm originally from Sante Fe. I was born there, I grew up there, and I went to school there. How about you?
   __1__ So, tell me a little about yourself.
   ___ Well . . . Are you originally from around here?
   ___ I was born right here in New York and lived here until I finished high school.

2. ___ I'm a lawyer. And you?
   ___ I have two brothers. They both live in Bangkok.
   ___ I'm a doctor.
   ___ In Bangkok? That's interesting. By the way, what do you do?
   ___ A doctor? That's interesting.
   ___ Yes. I have three brothers and a sister. They all live in Los Angeles. How about you?
   __1__ Tell me about your family. Do you have any brothers and sisters?

B. Listen

Listen and choose the correct response.

1. (a.) I don't know where to begin.
   b. Do you know?
2. a. Do you generally live here?
   b. Are you originally from around here?
3. a. I'm from Cleveland.
   b. Nice to meet you.
4. a. No, I'm not.
   b. Yes, I do.
5. a. I have a brother and a sister.
   b. By the way.
6. a. Yes. I have three sisters.
   b. No. I'm not married.
7. a. I don't.
   b. I'm an accountant.
8. a. I'm a teacher.
   b. That's interesting.

C. Open Road!

Tell a little about yourself and your family.

.....

.....

.....

D. What's the Word?

Complete the following.

invite	buying	see	do	relax	visit	wash	sleep
rake	prepare	look	go	read	eat	spend	

Many people _____ look _____ 1 forward to the weekend. They like to enjoy themselves and have fun. On Friday nights, many people like to _____ 2 at home after work and watch TV. Other people _____ 3 out for dinner or go to _____ 4 a movie.

On Saturdays, supermarkets and shopping malls are crowded with people _____ 5 food, clothing, or presents. Many people _____ 6 chores around the house on Saturday. They paint, _____ 7 leaves, _____ 8 their cars, and do laundry. On Saturday evenings, many people go out, _____ 9 people to come over for dinner, or _____ 10 friends.

On Sunday mornings, many people _____ 11 late. Some people go to church, _____ 12 the newspaper, and _____ 13 Sunday "brunch." On Sunday afternoons, many people have a big dinner and visit relatives. Other people _____ 14 Sunday afternoons at museums, theaters, and shopping malls. On Sunday evenings, people usually stay home and _____ 15 for the week ahead.

E. Listen

Listen and circle the word you hear.

1	(relax)	go back	4	chores	shores	7	visit	wish
2	father	brother	5	brush	brunch	8	watch	wash
3	day	play	6	zoo	soon	9	rock	lot

F. Matching Lines

Match the lines.

d	1 What's your favorite part of the week?	a. I'm a teacher.
___	2 Where did you grow up?	b. Sure. What?
___	3 I won a prize at the county fair.	c. I visit friends and watch TV.
___	4 My daughter broke up with her fiancé.	d. The weekend.
___	5 What do you do?	e. I heard it in the cafeteria.
___	6 Tell me about your family.	f. What a shame!
___	7 Are you positive?	g. Yes, I am.
___	8 Who told you that?	h. In Chicago.
___	9 Can I ask you something?	i. That's great!
___	10 What do you usually do to relax on the weekend?	j. I have one sister and three brothers.

G. Wrong Way!

Harry had an incredible weekend. What happened? Put the words in the correct order.

1 married On he afternoon girlfriend. his Friday

_____

2 lottery. they Saturday won the On in $10,000

_____

H. Open Road!

Tell about YOUR weekend.

.....

.....

Exit 3

Call Directory Assistance

Student Text Pages 36–37

A. Wrong Way!

Put the lines in the correct order.

___ Can you spell that?

___ Hmm. I'm pretty sure, but I'd better check. Thank you, Operator.

___ What street?

_1_ Directory assistance. What city?

___ Just a moment. . . . I'm sorry, but I don't have a Carl Morrison on Alamo Road. Are you certain you have the correct address?

___ M-O-R-R-I-S-O-N.

___ Alamo Road.

___ Dallas. I'd like the number of Carl Morrison.

B. Fill It In!

Fill in the correct answer.

1. Directory assistance. _____?
   a. What street?
   (b.) What city?

2. I'd like the number of _____.
   a. Middle Street
   b. Michael Gonzalez

3. Just a moment . . . _____.
   a. The number is 223-6710.
   b. The address is 45 Lantern Lane.

4. Are you certain you _____?
   a. have the correct number
   b. have the correct address

5. I'm pretty sure, but _____.
   a. I'd better check
   b. I'd better chest

6. Thank you, _____.
   a. Operation
   b. Operator

7. I'm sorry, but _____.
   a. I don't know a Joe Day at B Street
   b. I don't have a Joe Day on B Street

C. Listen

Listen and put a check next to the sentence you hear.

1. ✓ I hear about it every day.
   ___ I heard about it every day.

2. ___ Go to the corner and turn at the light.
   ___ Go to the corner and turn right.

3. ___ I walk to the store every day.
   ___ I work at the store every day.

4. ___ Do you have any plants?
   ___ Do you have any plans?

5. ___ That telephone number is long!
   ___ That telephone number is wrong!

6. ___ She wants to go to work tomorrow.
   ___ She won't go to work tomorrow.

7. ___ That teacher taught math.
   ___ That teacher thought about math.

8. ___ Sally won the race.
   ___ Sally was number eight.

D. Open Road!

Complete the conversation any way you wish.

A. Directory assistance. What city?

.....

B. I'd like the number of .....

A. Would you spell that?

B. .....

A. What street?

B. .....

A. Just a moment. The number is .....

B. Thank you, Operator.

E. Listen

Listen and write the spelling of each name.

1. L - A - W - L - E - R
2. ___-___-___-___
3. ___-___-___-___-___
4. ___-___-___-___-___-___-___
5. ___-___-___-___-___-___
6. ___-___-___-___-___-___-___

Make Telephone Calls

Student Text
Pages 38–39

A. The Right Choice

Circle the correct word.

A. Hello.

B. Hello. Dr. Ableman?

A. I'm [sure / (sorry)] [1]. There's [nobody / somebody] [2] here by that [number / name] [3].

B. Is [this / he] [4] 396-1136?

A. No, it [is / isn't] [5].

B. Oh. I [apologize / apology] [6]. I guess I [dial / dialed] [7] the wrong number.

B. Matching Lines

Match the questions and answers.

e	1 Is this 478-0092?	a. No, I don't.
___	2 Did they have a good day?	b. No, I'm not.
___	3 Do you have good news?	c. No, they weren't.
___	4 Are they from here?	d. No, it wasn't.
___	5 Was it easy?	e. No, it isn't.
___	6 Were your children at school yesterday?	f. No, he doesn't.
___	7 Does Bill drive to work every day?	g. No, they aren't.
___	8 Are you having trouble with this exercise?	h. No, they didn't.

C. What Are They Saying?

Choose the correct answer.

1. This person is ____.
   (a.) asking for information
   b. apologizing

2. This person is ____.
   a. apologizing
   b. reporting information

3. This person is ____.
   a. certain
   b. asking for information

4. This person is ____.
   a. certain
   b. uncertain

5. This person is ____.
   a. reporting information
   b. apologizing

6. This person is ____.
   a. almost positive
   b. not sure

D. Open Road!

Call a friend and report some good news.

A. Hello.

B. Hello, ...? This is .....
I have some good news to tell you.

A. What?

B. .....

A. That's .....!

Call a friend and report some bad news.

A. Hello.

B. Hello, ...? This is .....
I have some bad news to tell you.

A. What?

B. .....

A. That's .....!

Access Public Transportation

Student Text
Pages 40–43

A. The Right Choice

Circle the correct words.

A. Pardon me. Does this bus go to Las Vegas?

B. No, it (doesn't does)[1]. It goes to Seattle. You want the Nevada bus.

A. The Nevada bus?

B. (Yes No)[2].

A. (When Where)[3] can I get it?

B. It's at (pier gate)[4] 7.

A. (Thank you Excuse me)[5].

A. (Excuse me Thanks)[6]. Where can I get the 8:00 flight to Denver?

B. I'm (pardon sorry)[7], but that flight just left.

A. (Oh, yes Oh, no)[8]! I missed the flight?!

B. I'm afraid you did.

A. I can't believe it! (I got to I've got to)[9] get to a business meeting. When is the next flight?

B. (Let me see I don't believe)[10]. It's at 10:00. Will that get you to Denver in time for your business meeting?

A. (I hope so I need to)[11].

B. Sense or Nonsense?

Do each of the following "make sense" or are they "nonsense"?

	Sense	*Nonsense*
1 "You can get the ferry at pier 7."	✓	
2 "The bus to Washington is at gate 34."		
3 "The express train is on the expressway."		
4 "This monorail goes to the parking lot."		
5 "I can't believe it! I missed my ticket!"		
6 "You can buy your reunion right here."		

C. Crosswalk

ACROSS

5. I'm getting married. Today is my _____ day.
8. The _____ is at pier 4.
9. When I graduate from college, I'm going to my college _____.
10. Wait for the train on the other _____.

DOWN

1. I'm going to my high school _____.
2. The ship leaves from _____ 15.
3. I have bad news. I have to go to a _____.
4. This _____ goes to the Magic Kingdom.
6. Flight 754 leaves from _____ 2B.
7. The train to Las Vegas is on _____ 45.

D. WordRap: *Going Places!*

Listen. Then clap and practice.

A. Does this plane go to Timbuktu?
B. No, you want flight 402.

A. Does this bus stop in front of the store?
B. No, you want bus number 4.

A. Does this flight go to Santa Fe?
B. Yes, it does, but it's full today.

A. Is there a train to Idaho?
B. Yes, but it left an hour ago!

A. Where can I get bus 24?
B. Right over there, near the candy store.

A. Where can I find track number 3?
B. That's where I'm going. Just follow me.

Give Directions to Places in the Community

Student Text
Pages 44–47

A. The Right Choice

Circle the correct words.

A. Excuse me. (Could you tell me / Could you tell) [1] how to get to the City Park?

B. Yes. Drive down this road until you go to / get to [2] the next intersection. Turn right and drive two blocks. Turn left, and you'll see the park on the left.

A. I'm sorry. I didn't get that / I didn't say that [3]. Could you please remember / repeat [4] that?

B. Okay. First, go to the next car / corner [5] and turn right on Oak Street.

A. Okay.

B. Then drive two blocks, and turn left on Pine Street.

Are you with me / Are you follow me [6] so far?

A. Yes. I don't understand / understand [7].

B. You'll see the park on the left. Have you got all that?

A. Yes, now I got it / I've got it [8]. Thanks very much.

B. You're welcome.

B. The 5th Wheel!

Which one doesn't belong?

1 Okay.	Sure.	I'm sorry.	All right.
2 Excuse me.	I'm following you.	I'm with you.	I understand.
3 I apologize.	That's right.	Excuse me.	I'm sorry.
4 I've got to	I want to	I have to	I need to
5 Okay so far?	I didn't follow you.	I didn't get that.	I don't understand.
6 Are you there?	Can you tell me?	Do you know?	Could you tell me?
7 Are you sure?	Are you certain?	Are you positive?	Do you know?
8 Uh-húh.	I didn't follow you.	That's right.	Yes.

C. Listen

Look at the map and listen to the directions. If the directions are correct, write **C**. If they are incorrect, write **I**.

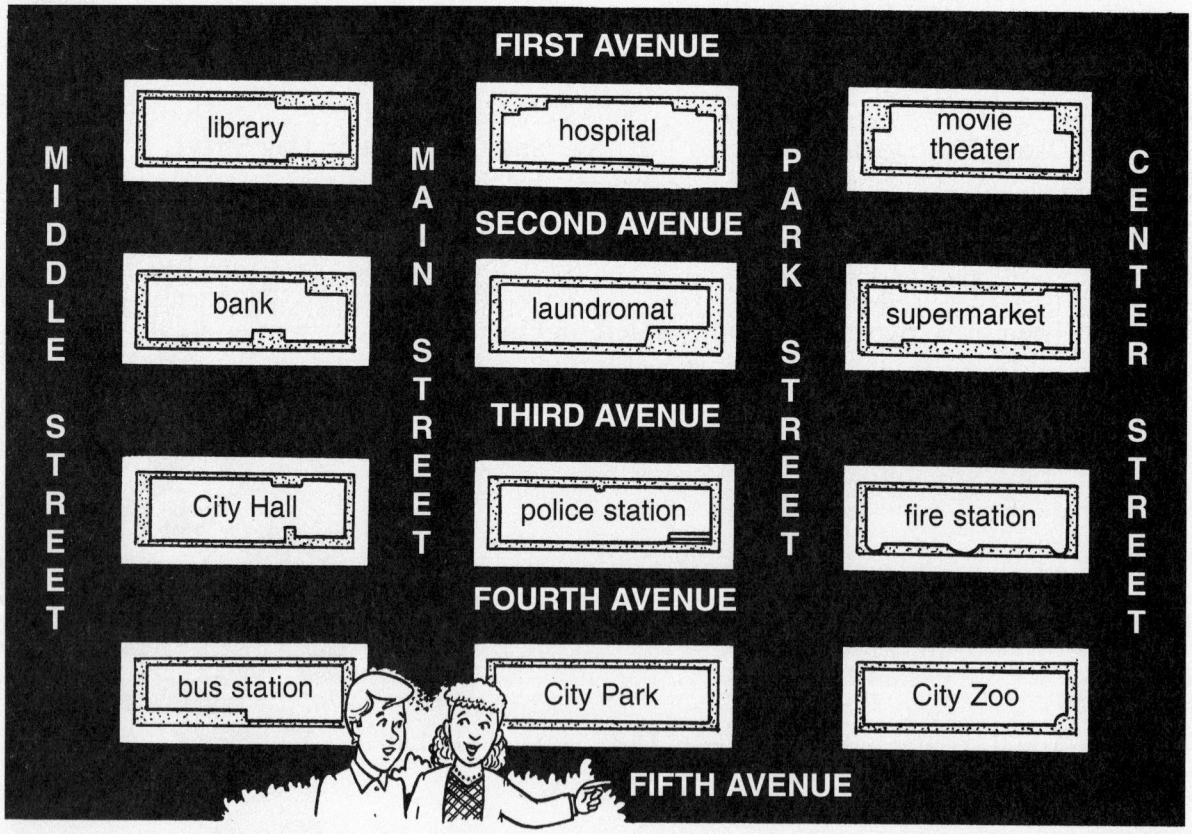

1 C
2 ___
3 ___
4 ___
5 ___
6 ___
7 ___
8 ___
9 ___

D. What's the Line?

Complete the conversation any way you wish.

A. ..... 1 how to get to the university?

B. Yes. Walk to the corner and turn right. Walk two blocks to Elm Street and turn left. Walk three more blocks, and you'll see the university on the left.

A. I'm sorry. I didn't get that. ..... 2 ?

B. Sure. First, walk to the corner and turn right.

A. ..... 3 .

B. Then walk two blocks to Elm Street and turn left. ..... 4 ?

A. Yes. I'm following you.

B. Then walk three more blocks, and you'll see the university on the left. Have you got all that?

A. Yes. ..... 5 .
Thanks very much.

E. What's the Response?

Choose the correct response.

1. Excuse me. Do you know how to get to the park?
   a. Yes, there's a park.
   (b.) Yes, I do.

2. Go to the next corner and turn right.
   a. Turn the right corner?
   b. Turn at the next corner?

3. Yes. Turn right onto Oakland Avenue.
   a. Um-hmm.
   b. Do you repeat that?

4. Walk along Oakland Avenue a few blocks.
   a. Okay.
   b. I'll see.

5. You'll see the park on the left.
   a. I didn't know.
   b. On the left?

6. Yes. It's on the left, next to the museum.
   a. Park next to the museum?
   b. The park is next to the museum?

7. Yes. It's on the left, next to the museum.
   a. Now I'm with you.
   b. Now I'm so far.

8. Have you got all that?
   a. Yes. All right.
   b. Yes. Now I've got it.

Give Directions for Traveling by Car

Student Text
Pages 48–51

A. Wrong Way!

Put the lines in the correct order.

___ Betty! Where ARE you?

___ Oh. That's the problem. You were supposed to get off at Exit 25.

___ I'm afraid I am.

1 Hello.

___ I think so. I took Maple Street to Fourth Avenue. Then I turned left and took the Interstate south to Exit 27.

___ You're lost?!

___ Tell me, Betty, where are you now?

7 Did you follow my directions?

___ Hello, Maria? This is Betty.

___ I'm calling from a phone at Denny's Donuts.

___ Exit 25?! Oh.

___ You won't believe it! I'm lost!

___ Oh, that's not far from here. Here's what you should do.

B. Matching Lines

Match the lines.

b 1 Drive about three miles and you'll see a large ____.

___ 2 You'll see my house at the end of the ____.

___ 3 Follow Madison Street for two ____.

___ 4 Drive to the corner and turn ____.

___ 5 Take a right on Washington ____.

___ 6 You didn't follow my ____.

___ 7 Go north on the ____.

___ 8 Get off at Exit ____.

a. blocks
b. sign
c. interstate
d. directions
e. left
f. block
g. Boulevard
h. 15

C. What's the Word?

Complete the sentences.

commuters	honk	midday	rush	underground	carpools
intersection	hail	traffic	sites	highways	ancient

1. In Athens and Rome, they can't build new ___highways___ because of the historic sites.
2. In many cities, there are special lanes for _____ of three or more people.
3. The time of the day when people go to work and come home from work is called _____ hour.
4. In some countries, many workers go home for a _____ break.
5. Many people in Seoul stand at intersections and _____ a cab.
6. Some people _____ their horns when there is a lot of traffic.
7. The subway systems in Tokyo and Rome are _____.
8. The Forum and the Colosseum are historic _____.
9. The city streets are full of _____ at rush hour.
10. An _____ is the place where two streets meet.
11. Heavy _____ is a problem in many cities.
12. An old city is an _____ city.

D. The 5th Wheel!

Which one doesn't belong?

1	ancient	old	historic	(artifacts)
2	automobiles	mopeds	subways	city
3	carpool	highway	intersection	street
4	build	make	hail	construct
5	Athens	Canada	Seoul	Rome
6	archeologists	artifacts	ancient	normal
7	trains	packers	commuters	cab drivers
8	gate	track	moped	pier
9	ferry	pier	bus	plane
10	lunch	wedding	funeral	graduation

E. Word Search

Find 7 ways to get to and from work.

P	D	G	C	L	O	U	T	L	S	I	F	Z	B	B	O
E	B	U	C	E	S	L	X	T	A	X	Y	W	A	Y	A
T	I	B	B	I	L	T	P	H	T	A	X	I	S	C	M
R	P	I	T	A	R	T	O	M	O	B	O	D	G	S	U
C	L	C	A	N	A	W	A	T	L	U	P	B	U	O	A
P	I	Y	K	U	I	A	N	N	S	V	P	T	N	P	U
O	P	C	E	P	M	A	U	T	O	M	A	T	I	C	T
W	R	L	O	P	E	B	U	S	E	S	H	K	Z	C	O
E	T	E	U	P	S	A	I	S	C	U	T	D	O	W	M
G	J	S	R	L	X	N	N	W	E	T	U	O	S	P	O
L	D	R	H	Y	N	G	L	X	Z	W	M	O	N	C	B
A	E	N	L	A	Z	Y	O	U	B	I	O	H	A	P	I
X	G	S	U	B	W	A	Y	S	U	B	P	E	D	S	L
P	I	D	S	G	I	V	S	E	C	I	E	S	B	U	E
B	B	A	Y	H	I	G	H	W	C	C	D	F	R	G	S
T	R	A	I	N	S	U	T	D	O	W	S	A	W	A	T

F. Listen

Listen to the traffic report and choose the correct answers.

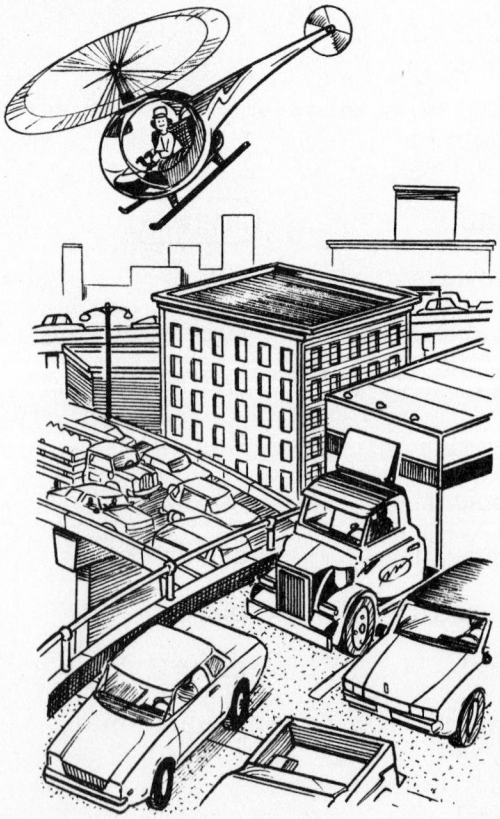

1. a. There's an accident on the subway.
   b. There's an accident on the highway.
   c. Commuters should take the highway to work.
   d. Commuters should take the subway to work.
2. a. The trains are very slow this morning.
   b. The buses are very fast this morning.
   c. Commuters should take the bus.
   d. Commuters should take taxis.
3. a. It's snowing. The trains and buses are late.
   b. It's snowing. The trains and taxis are late.
   c. Getting to work will be difficult.
   d. Getting home from work will be difficult.
4. a. There's good news for commuters today.
   b. There's good news for computers today.
   c. The new subway system is open.
   d. The new taxi system is open.

Check-Up Test: Exits 1, 2, 3

A. What's the Word?

Complete the sentences.

Who	What	Where	When	Which	Why	Whose	How

1. A. What did you do last night?
   B. I invited people over for dinner.
2. A. _____ long are you going to stay?
   B. A few days.
3. A. _____ school do you go to?
   B. Burbank High School.
4. A. _____ understands the homework?
   B. Mary does.
5. A. _____ cake won first prize?
   B. Marvin Crawford's cake.
6. A. Excuse me. _____ is the ferry to Manhattan?
   B. It's at pier 7.
7. A. _____ is your birthday?
   B. It's July 15th.
8. A. _____ did they lay off the workers?
   B. There wasn't any work.

B. Listen

Listen and circle the word you hear.

1	(went)	want	5	heard	overheard	9	go	know
2	wreck	wrecked	6	let	left	10	went	rent
3	dial	dialed	7	died	die	11	heard	hear
4	find	found	8	believed	believe	12	gave	gives

C. Matching Lines

Match the lines.

d	1 Is this 465-7798?	a. No. He's going to retire.
___	2 Are you Greek?	b. Yes, you did.
___	3 Could you please repeat that?	c. Yes, he was.
___	4 Did I call at a bad time?	d. No, it isn't.
___	5 Can I ask you a question?	e. No. I'm Italian.
___	6 Is the boss going to quit?	f. Sure. What is it?
___	7 Was your son-in-law at home when you called?	g. Sure. Walk three blocks to Main Street.

D. Same or Different?

Is the meaning the same or different?

1. "Nice to meet you."
   "That's wonderful!"
   same (*different*)

2. "No, actually not."
   "Not really."
   same *different*

3. "That's too bad!"
   "That's fantastic!"
   same *different*

4. "Can you tell me how to get there?"
   "Do you know how to get there?"
   same *different*

5. "Where did you hear that?"
   "I don't believe it!"
   same *different*

6. "Excuse me."
   "Pardon me."
   same *different*

7. "I've got to go."
   "I need to go."
   same *different*

8. "Could you please repeat that?"
   "Could you please say that again?"
   same *different*

9. "Where are your things?"
   "How are things?"
   same *different*

10. "Are you with me so far?"
    "Are you following me so far?"
    same *different*

E. What's the Word?

Complete the sentences.

aren't	wasn't	weren't	don't	doesn't	didn't

1. My mother-in-law __didn't__ arrive yesterday.
2. Jennifer _____ want to move to another city.
3. The rush hour traffic _____ a problem last night. It was Saturday.
4. I'm sorry. We _____ have any rooms.
5. It's very cold today. The boys _____ going to go skiing.
6. We _____ very lucky yesterday. We got a speeding ticket.

F. The 5th Wheel!

Which one doesn't belong?

1	where	what	why	(wheel)	who
2	mother	brother	nephew	husband	father
3	Swedes	Koreans	Spaniards	Brazil	Japanese
4	pier	gate	track	platform	door
5	get a raise	win a prize	get fired	win the lottery	get a promotion

Exit 4

Describe Features of an Apartment

Student Text Pages 56–59

A. The Right Choice

Circle the correct word.

A. (Where (How))[1] can I help you?

B. We're looking for a two-bedroom (department apartment)[2] near public transportation.

A. Hmm. I think I have just what you're (looking for looking at)[3].

B. Oh, good. (What Where)[4] is it?

A. It's on Porter Avenue.

B. What kind of (neighbor neighborhood)[5] is it?

A. It's very (safe safely)[6].

B. That sounds good. What can you (tell say)[7] us about the apartment?

A. Well, you'll love the kitchen! It has brand new (cabinets stove)[8]!

B. Hmm. Another question. (Do Are)[9] cats allowed in the building?

A. Cats? Yes, I believe they (do are)[10].

B. How (large much)[11] is the rent?

A. $850 a month.

B. (Are Does)[12] that include utilities?

A. Everything except (electricity utilities)[13].

B. Matching Lines

Match the abbreviations and the words.

c	1	conv.	a.	electricity	___	7	a/c	g.	transportation
___	2	mo.	b.	including	___	8	loc.	h.	fireplace
___	3	incl.	c.	convenient	___	9	utils.	i.	air conditioning
___	4	w/	d.	building	___	10	lge.	j.	location
___	5	bldg.	e.	month	___	11	fpl.	k.	large
___	6	elec.	f.	with	___	12	trans.	l.	utilities

C. Listen

Listen and circle the word you hear.

1	three-bedroom	two-bedroom	7	driver	dryer
2	in town	downtown	8	included	including
3	$560	$650	9	near	close
4	electricity	utilities	10	talking	walking
5	beds	pets	11	neighborhood	neighbors
6	desire	quiet	12	rules	dues

D. Crosswalk

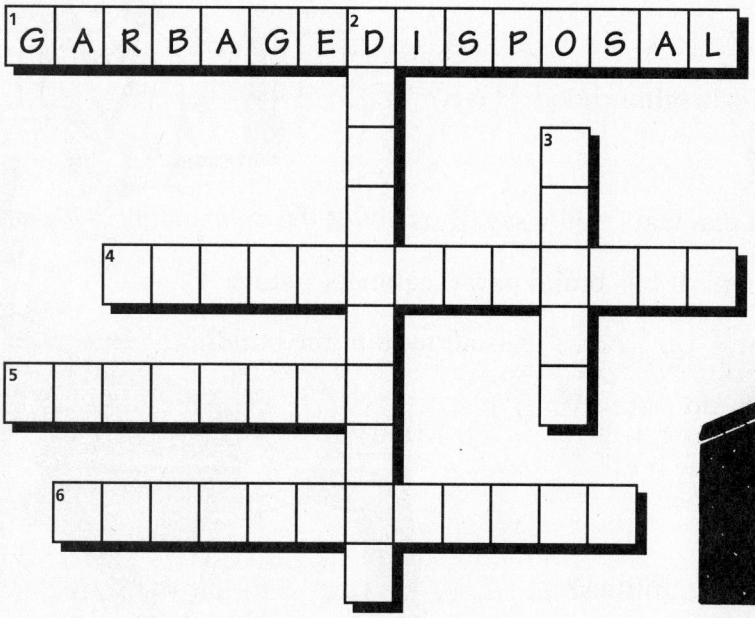

E. Matching Lines

Make associations.

c	1 waterbed	a.	kitchen	___	7 gas	g.	living room
___	2 one-bedroom	b.	location	___	8 fireplace	h.	neighborhood
___	3 dog	c.	bedroom	___	9 polite	i.	utilities
___	4 desirable	d.	apartment	___	10 6th floor	j.	rent
___	5 dishwasher	e.	transportation	___	11 $975	k.	neighbors
___	6 bus	f.	pet	___	12 safe	l.	building

Enumerate Food Items

Student Text
Pages 60–63

A. Wrong Way!

Put the lines in the correct order.

____ Okay. Anything else besides the yogurt and the onions?

____ Four small containers. I guess we also need a few onions.

____ All right. What do you want me to get?

____ Let me think. How about three?

__1__ Could you do me a favor?

____ Yes. We're out of bread.

____ Well, could you pick up some yogurt?

____ How many should I get?

____ Certainly. What is it?

____ I think one loaf will be enough.

____ Could you run over to the store? We need a few things.

____ Some yogurt? Sure. How much?

____ Okay. How much bread do you want me to get?

____ Okay. So that's four small containers of yogurt, three onions, and a loaf of bread.

B. Listen

Listen and choose the correct response.

1. a. Let me think.
   (b.) Sure.
2. a. Thanks a lot.
   b. All right.
3. a. The store.
   b. Some ground beef.
4. a. Okay. How much?
   b. Okay. How many?
5. a. A small bunch.
   b. A small head.
6. a. Half a pound.
   b. Half a gallon.
7. a. Okay.
   b. I think so.
8. a. A bottle.
   b. A few cans.
9. a. Mineral water.
   b. White bread.
10. a. Yes. A big stick.
    b. Yes. A big tube.
11. a. A 4-ounce quart.
    b. A 4-ounce jar.
12. a. Yes. A pint.
    b. Yes. A pound.

C. Fill It In!

Fill in the correct answer.

1. We need _____ eggs.
   a. a pound of
   (b.) a dozen

2. Could you pick up _____ of milk?
   a. a quart
   b. a box

3. We need _____ of butter.
   a. two gallons
   b. two sticks

4. Please get _____ of orange juice.
   a. a tube
   b. a half gallon

5. We need _____ of peanut butter.
   a. a jar
   b. a bottle

6. Could you get _____ crackers?
   a. a box
   b. some

7. Could you pick up _____ lemons?
   a. three large
   b. a small jar of

8. Please get _____ of soda.
   a. half a dozen
   b. two six-packs

9. We need _____ of lettuce.
   a. a head
   b. a loaf

10. Let's get _____ of tuna fish.
    a. a box
    b. a few cans

11. Please pick up _____ avocados.
    a. a head of
    b. two or three

12. We also need _____ toothpaste.
    a. a small
    b. a tube

D. WordRap: *Shopping List*

Listen. Then clap and practice.

A. We need a loaf of bread.
B. Whole wheat or white?
A. I like whole wheat,
But white's all right.

A. Could you pick up some apples
And a bunch of grapes?
B. We also need cheese
And some blank cassette tapes.

A. We're out of milk
And ice cream, too.
B. Should I pick up some yogurt?
A. Yes. Please do!

A. We need some lettuce
And a pound of rice.
B. How about some onions?
A. That would be nice!

Locate Items in a Supermarket

Student Text Pages 64–65

A. Wrong Way!

Put the lines in the correct order.

___ No, "7."

___ I'm sorry. Did you say "Aisle 11"?

___ Any time.

_1_ Pardon me. Where can I find toothpicks?

___ Oh. Thanks a lot.

___ Toothpicks? They're in the Paper Products Section, Aisle 7.

B. What's the Line?

Complete the conversations.

1. A. Where can I find TV dinners?
   B. They're in the Frozen Food Section, Aisle 3.

2. A. Where can I find milk?
   B. _____

3. A. Where can I find tortillas?
   B. _____

4. A. Where can I find ice cream?
   B. _____

5. A. Pardon me. Where's the lettuce?
   B. _____

6. A. Where can I find toothpicks?
   B. _____

7. A. Excuse me. Where are the sponges?
   B. _____

8. A. Pardon me. Where's the cheese?
   B. _____

C. Listen

Listen and choose the correct line to complete the conversation.

1. (a.) Yes. Aisle A.
   b. No. Aisle J.
2. a. Yes. "G."
   b. No. "J."
3. a. Yes. Aisle 9.
   b. No. Aisle 5.
4. a. Yes. Aisle B.
   b. Yes. Aisle C.
5. a. No. "N."
   b. No. "M."
6. a. Yes. Aisle 7.
   b. Yes. Aisle 11.

D. Mystery Products!

Unscramble each of these items. Where can you find them at the supermarket?

Dairy	Household Supplies	Paper Products
Frozen Food	Imported Foods	Produce

1. p n e s o g s ___sponges___ Look in the ___Household Supplies___ Section.
2. a s t t m o o e _____ Look in the _____ Section.
3. m k s i m k l i _____ Look in the _____ Section.
4. p s i n k a n _____ Look in the _____ Section.
5. z o r f n e a p s e _____ Look in the _____ Section.
6. o c t a h s s l e l _____ Look in the _____ Section.

E. The 5th Wheel!

Which one doesn't belong?

1	(rice)	whole wheat bread	white bread	raisin bread
2	eggs	lemons	yogurt	Swiss cheese
3	sponges	napkins	toothpicks	peanut butter
4	chicken	onions	ground beef	lamb chops
5	check cashing	coffee	film developing	lottery tickets
6	tuna fish	avocados	peppers	potatoes
7	TV dinners	mayonnaise	ice cream	frozen yogurt
8	apples	butter	oranges	bananas
9	taco shells	tortillas	chili peppers	bug spray
10	toothpaste	cookies	cake	sugar

Evaluate the Cost of Food Items

Student Text
Pages 66–67

A. Matching Lines

Which lines have the same meaning?

c 1

___ 2

___ 3

___ 4

___ 5

a. "I agree with you."

b. "I'm really surprised."

c. "That's the cost."

d. "Is that the correct amount?"

e. "I think that's expensive."

B. Matching Prices

Match the prices.

e 1 thirteen dollars and forty-five cents

___ 2 thirty-two dollars and twelve cents

___ 3 nineteen dollars and thirty-six cents

___ 4 twenty dollars and ten cents

___ 5 four dollars and sixty-one cents

___ 6 fifty-four dollars and fifteen cents

___ 7 seventeen dollars and sixteen cents

___ 8 one hundred dollars and one cent

___ 9 fifty-four dollars and fifty cents

___ 10 eight dollars and seventy-nine cents

___ 11 ten dollars and twenty-three cents

a. $100.01

b. $19.36

c. $8.79

d. $54.50

e. $13.45

f. $10.23

g. $20.10

h. $54.15

i. $4.61

j. $17.16

k. $32.12

C. Believable or Unbelievable?

Are the following prices "believable" or "unbelievable"?

	Believable	*Unbelievable*
1 "A jar of peanut butter is about $2.00."	✓	
2 "You can get a new car for $1,000.00."		
3 "A newspaper costs about $10.00."		
4 "CDs are sometimes on sale for $10.99."		
5 "Napkins cost about $1.50."		
6 "You can get a pound of cheese for $3.00."		
7 "A new house costs about $900.00."		
8 "A two-bedroom apartment costs $800.00 a month."		
9 "A half gallon of milk costs about $.07."		
10 "You can get a dozen eggs for about $111.20."		

D. Listen

Listen and circle the correct price.

1	twelve fifteen	(twelve fifty)	6	thirteen thirty	thirty thirteen
2	ten forty-five	ten fifty-four	7	one ninety-nine	one eighty-nine
3	two forty	two fifty	8	nineteen cents	ninety cents
4	six sixty-seven	six seventy-six	9	three eighteen	three eighty
5	twelve twenty-five	twelve twenty	10	one seventeen	one seventy

E. Open Road!

Write a shopping list for yourself. What do you think each item will cost?

Item	*Cost?*

Discuss Ingredients

Student Text
Pages 68–69

A. The Right Choice

Circle the correct words.

A. Mmm. (These are This is)[1] superb!
What (is it are they)[2]?

B. (It's They're)[3] pancakes.

A. Pancakes?

B. Yes. (They're It's)[4] a popular American dish.

A. Well, (they're it's)[5] wonderful. What's in (it them)[6]?

B. Let me see . . . a (few little)[7] flour, a (few little)[8] water, a (few little)[9] eggs, and . . . uh, oh yes, a (few little)[10] milk.

A. (Are they Is it)[11] difficult to make?

B. No, not at all. I'll be happy to give you the recipe.

A. Mmm. (These are This is)[12] delicious!
What (is it are they)[13]?

B. (They're It's)[14] lasagna.

A. Lasagna?

B. Yes. (They're It's)[15] a popular Italian dish.

A. Well, (it's they're)[16] fantastic! What's in (them it)[17]?

B. Let me see . . . a (few little)[18] ground beef, a (little few)[19] tomato sauce, and a (few little)[20] cheese.

A. (Is it Are they)[21] difficult to make?

B. No, not at all. I'll be happy to give you the recipe.

B. Open Road!

Tell about a new food you tried. What was it? What were the ingredients? Did you like it?

.....

.....

C. Listen

Do you remember the ingredients of the foods on student text page 68? Listen and write the number under the correct food.

borscht ____

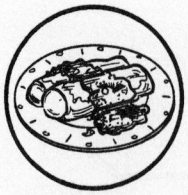

manicotti 1

enchiladas ____

moussaka ____

egg rolls ____

D. What's the Word?

Complete the conversations.

it	them	sugar	ground beef	tomatoes	apples	chocolate	lettuce	eggs

E. What's the Question?

Write the questions.

1. What are they ? — They're tacos.
2. _____? — It's a peanut butter sandwich.
3. _____? — No, not at all. They're easy to make.
4. _____? — A few onions and a little sour cream.

Give Recipe Instructions

Student Text
Pages 70-73

A. What's the Response?

Choose the correct response.

1. Your beef stew was fantastic!
   a. Yes. I'm with you.
   (b.) Oh, did you really like it?

2. Did you like it?
   a. Very much.
   b. Thank you very much.

3. It was superb!
   a. Could you repeat?
   b. Thank you for saying so.

4. Now I've got it. Is that it?
   a. That's it!
   b. I'll say!

5. Are you following me so far?
   a. Yes, I'm following with you.
   b. Yes, I'm with you.

6. Could I ask for the recipe?
   a. I'm sure.
   b. Sure.

7. Is it easy?
   a. It's really very easy.
   b. It's really excellent.

8. Thanks very much.
   a. You can say that again!
   b. My pleasure.

B. Sense or Nonsense?

Do the following "make sense" or are they "nonsense"?

	Sense	*Nonsense*
1. "Supermarkets sell vending machines."	_____	✓
2. "Ice cream is in the Frozen Food Section."	_____	_____
3. "Butchers work in bakeries."	_____	_____
4. "Money machines in supermarkets make money."	_____	_____
5. "Some supermarkets have snack bars."	_____	_____
6. "Shampoo is in the Health Care Products Section."	_____	_____
7. "Some supermarkets are enormous."	_____	_____
8. "Fish markets sell screwdrivers and hammers."	_____	_____
9. "You can buy ground beef at a butcher shop."	_____	_____
10. "Look for cheese in the Dairy Section."	_____	_____
11. "Specialty stores are for special people."	_____	_____
12. "Neighborhood grocery stores are always larger than supermarkets."	_____	_____

C. Fill It In!

Fill in the correct answer.

1. I need a bunch of _____.
   a. grapes
   b. mineral water

2. Please buy two tubes of _____.
   a. potato chips
   b. toothpaste

3. We need a liter of _____.
   a. eggs
   b. apple juice

4. Please get a few bags of _____.
   a. popcorn
   b. mayonnaise

5. Don't forget to buy a head of _____.
   a. lettuce
   b. peanut butter

6. I need a pound of _____.
   a. cereal
   b. ground beef

7. Please buy three cans of _____.
   a. baked beans
   b. mustard

8. Pick up a six-pack of _____.
   a. cinnamon
   b. soda

D. What's the Word?

Complete the recipe.

some	few	little	Cut up	Put	Add	Mix	Bake	Serve

Bob's Chicken Delight

Cut up [1] _____ [2] pieces of chicken, a _____ [3] tomatoes, and _____ [4] onions. _____ [5] the chicken, the tomatoes, and the onions into a pan with a _____ [6] salt. _____ [7] together a _____ [8] flour and _____ [9] water. _____ [10] a _____ [11] pepper to the flour and water. _____ [12] the mixture into the pan with the chicken, the tomatoes, the onions, and the salt. _____ [13] for two hours at 325 degrees. _____ [14] with a _____ [15] rolls and a _____ [16] salad. Enjoy!

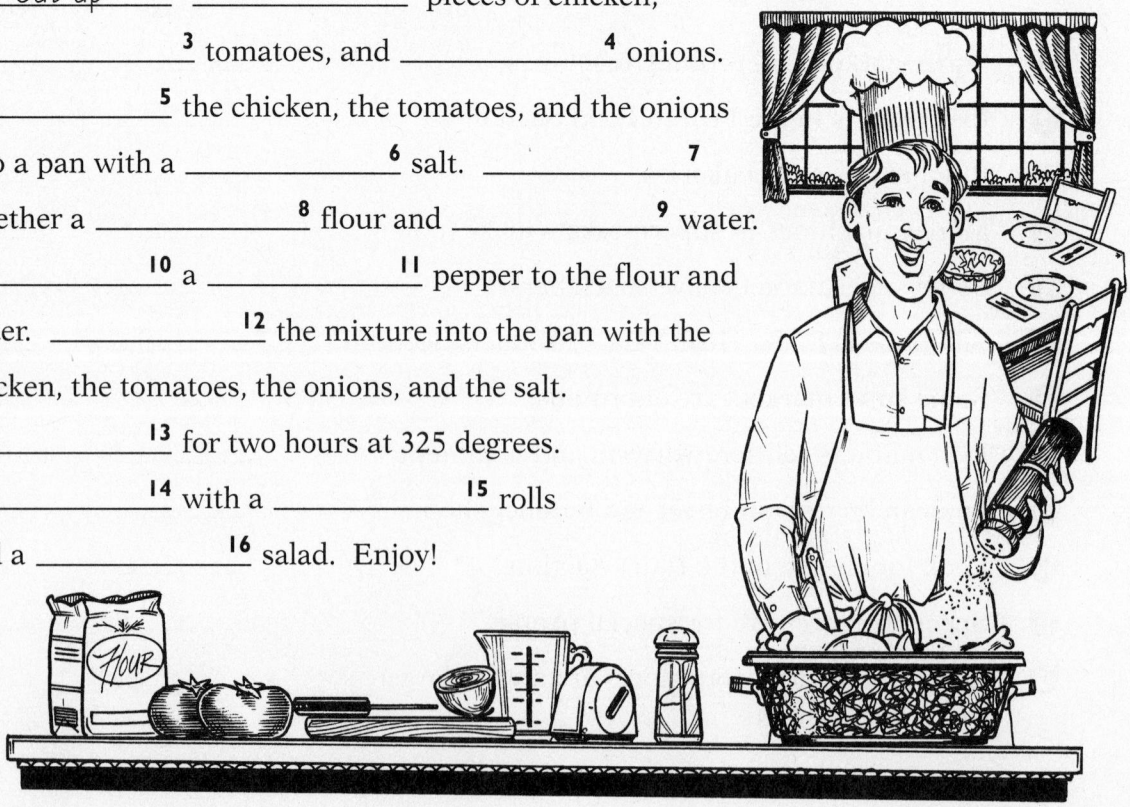

Exit 5

Tell About Work Skills

Student Text Pages 76–77

A. What's the Word?

Complete the conversation.

we're	do	fill	I've	I'd	done	saw	sit	have

A. I _____ saw _____ 1 your sign in the window.
What position _____ 2 you have open?

B. _____ 3 looking for a mechanic's assistant.

A. _____ 4 like to apply.

B. _____ 5 you _____ 6 engine tune-ups before?

A. Yes, I _____ 7. _____ 8 _____ 9 engine tune-ups in my last two jobs.

B. Okay. Here's an application form. You can _____ 10 over there and _____ 11 it out.

A. Thank you.

B. Fill It In!

Fill in the correct answer.

1. I _____ in my present job.
   a. written advertisments
   (b.) write advertisments

2. _____ in my last two jobs.
   a. I've taken inventory
   b. I take inventory

3. I _____ in my last job.
   a. wrote obituaries
   b. write obituaries

4. I know how to _____.
   a. done tune-ups
   b. do tune-ups

5. _____ pizza in my present job.
   a. I'd made
   b. I make

6. _____ in my last three jobs.
   a. I've driven a bus
   b. I'd driven a bus

Tell About Work-Related Events

Student Text
Pages 78-79

A. The Right Choice

Circle the correct word.

A. Is / Has (1) the manager gone / go (2) to the vault already / yet (3) ?

B. Yes, she has / is (4) . She's / She (5) yet / already (6) go / gone (7) there.

A. Oh, good. What / When (8) ?

B. She gone / went (9) there a little while ago.

A. Have / Did (10) you eat / eaten (11) in the new cafeteria yet / already (12) ?

B. Yes, I have / do (13) . I've / You've (14) already / yet (15) eat / eaten (16) there.

A. What / When (17) ?

B. I ate / eaten (18) there at lunch time.

The food was great!

B. What's the Line?

Complete the conversations.

1. A. Has Carol given her presentation yet?
   B. Yes. She's already given it. She gave it this morning.
2. A. Have the clerks gotten their raises yet?
   B. Yes. _____ already _____ them. _____ them yesterday.
3. A. Have you and Susan seen the report yet?
   B. Yes. _____ already _____ it. _____ it this morning.
4. A. Has David read his new contract yet?
   B. Yes. _____ already _____ it. _____ it a little while ago.
5. A. Gloria, have you met the new supervisor yet?
   B. Yes. _____ already _____ her. _____ her the other day.

C. Listen

Listen and circle the word you hear.

1	(wore)	worn	4	spoke	spoken	7	do	done
2	written	write	5	meet	met	8	seen	see
3	made	make	6	eaten	eat	9	take	taken

D. WordRap: *Work Talk!*

Listen. Then clap and practice.

A. Has he finished the report yet?
B. I don't know.
A. When did he start it?
B. An hour ago.

A. Has she gotten a raise?
B. It's hard to say.
She wouldn't tell me,
Anyway!

A. Have they moved their office?
Are they still in the city?
B. They moved to the suburbs.
It's very pretty.

A. Have you met the new boss?
Does he seem okay?
B. He seems all right.
But it's hard to say.

Tell About Accomplishments and Experiences

Student Text Pages 80-81

A. The Right Choice

Circle the correct word.

1. I've known how to use a computer (for (since)) 1990.
2. I've been interested in needlepoint (for since) the last few years.
3. I've gotten a promotion every year (for since) the past five years.
4. We've been English teachers at this school (for since) last year.
5. I've eaten at the Ling Garden restaurant (for since) many years.

B. Is or Has?

Check "is" or "has."

	is	*has*
1. He's known English for many years.		✓
2. He's traveling to Asia this summer.	✓	
3. She's learning to use a computer.		
4. It's been cold this winter.		
5. He's been interested in music since he was a child.		
6. There's an interesting museum near here.		
7. Where's he been?		
8. It's cold this winter.		
9. He's driven a truck since 1995.		
10. It's taken three hours to get home.		
11. She's already seen the newspaper today.		
12. She's happy to be on vacation.		
13. When's the concert?		
14. He's read the new contract.		
15. It's been a long hot summer!		
16. She's known my family for many years.		
17. There's a call for you on line 5.		
18. He's sung his last finale.		

C. Word Search

Find 8 past participles.

E	R	P	I	T	A	S	U	N	G	N	B	O	D	G	S	E	B
T	D	L	C	A	N	A	W	A	T	L	U	P	B	U	O	A	U
U	O	I	Y	K	U	I	A	N	N	R	E	A	D	N	P	T	A
L	N	P	R	E	P	M	A	T	T	O	R	A	T	I	C	E	E
Y	E	R	E	O	P	E	H	I	P	S	F	H	K	Z	C	N	M
Q	E	T	A	U	P	S	A	I	S	C	P	T	D	B	W	N	P
D	G	J	S	R	L	X	N	N	W	M	T	H	O	S	P	O	R
K	L	D	R	H	Y	N	G	L	X	Z	W	M	O	N	C	B	E
R	S	E	E	N	A	Z	Y	O	U	B	I	O	Q	A	X	N	A
A	X	G	S	U	G	O	N	E	S	U	B	R	E	D	S	L	A
O	P	I	D	S	G	O	T	T	E	N	E	E	S	B	U	E	S
U	B	B	A	Y	H	I	G	H	W	C	E	T	F	R	G	S	L
E	A	T	T	E	N	S	U	T	D	O	N	S	A	W	A	T	J

D. Listen

These people are talking at a high school reunion. Listen and put a check next to the things they've done.

✔ He's written several books.

___ He's been a teacher.

___ He's been a counselor.

___ He's eaten unusual foods.

___ He's traveled to many places.

___ She's studied the banjo.

___ She's studied the piano.

___ She's given ballet lessons.

___ She's sung opera.

___ She's sung with a rock band.

E. Open Road!

How about you? What have YOU done in the past few years?

I've .....

I've .....

I've .....

Express Confidence About Your Abilities

Student Text Pages 82-83

A. Wrong Way!

Put the lines in the correct order.

___ Do you really think so?

1 Have you ever sold computers?

___ Oh, yes. I'm a hundred percent sure.

___ No, I haven't, but I've sold stereo equipment, and I'm confident I could learn to sell computers very easily.

B. Matching Lines

Match the questions and answers.

e	1 Are you certain about that?	a. Yes, we have.
___	2 Has your daughter ever taken ballet lessons?	b. Yes, he has.
___	3 Have we ever gone to a nightclub?	c. No, she hasn't.
___	4 Have you ever wanted to sell cars?	d. No, they haven't.
___	5 Has your husband ever ridden a motorcycle?	e. I'm positive.
___	6 Have your parents ever been to China?	f. Yes, you have.
___	7 Have I asked too many questions?	g. No, I haven't.

C. Analogies

1. sing : sang *as* meet : met
2. write : written *as* eat : _____
3. took : taken *as* drove : _____
4. give : gave *as* do : _____
5. went : gone *as* spoke : _____
6. fly : flown *as* ride : _____
7. knew : known *as* got : _____
8. wear : worn *as* read : _____

D. Listen

Listen and circle the word you hear.

1	have	(has)	haven't	hasn't
2	have	has	haven't	hasn't
3	have	has	haven't	hasn't
4	have	has	haven't	hasn't
5	have	has	haven't	hasn't
6	have	has	haven't	hasn't

Discuss Job Performance

Student Text
Pages 84-85

A. The Right Choice

Circle the correct words.

A. Have you (repair (repaired))[1] the van yet?

B. No, I (haven't didn't)[2]. I was (thinking to going to)[3] do it this afternoon.

A. Would you (peace please)[4] do it as soon as possible? The van is supposed to be (repair repaired)[5] by 2 o'clock.

B. I'm sorry. (I didn't known that I didn't know that)[6]. I'll do it right away.

B. What's the Word?

Complete the sentences.

set	write	oil	polished	filled out	make	getting	fix
clean	typed	fed	arrange	vacuum	given out	spoken	eaten

1. Have you *given out* the paychecks yet?
2. Have you _____ in the cafeteria yet?
3. Please _____ all the rugs in the office.
4. Are you _____ the mail before lunch?
5. Have you _____ to your supervisor yet?
6. I _____ the tables in the lobby yesterday.
7. Have you _____ your time sheet for this week?
8. Please _____ the conveyer belt before every shift.
9. Have you _____ all the letters for Mr. Montenegro?
10. Will you please _____ the flowers after your break?
11. The animals are supposed to be _____ at 11 o'clock sharp.
12. You're supposed to _____ the animal cages every morning.
13. We're planning to _____ the tables an hour before we open.
14. The Zorax Company is supposed to _____ the copy machine.
15. Can you please _____ all the beds the first thing in the morning?
16. I'd like you to _____ your monthly report by the last day of the month.

Tell About Work Experience

Student Text
Pages 86-87

A. The Right Choice

Circle the correct words.

A. Are you able to sing and dance?

B. Yes. (We've been / We're) [1] singing and dancing (for / since) [2] a long time.

A. (For long / How long) [3] ?

B. (Since / For) [4] we were teenagers.

A. (Since you were teenagers / Since we were teenagers) [5] ?

B. Yes, (that's right / that right) [6] .

A. Well, you certainly have a lot of experience.

B. I guess we do.

B. Listen

Which sentence do you hear?

1. (a.) I've been using the Internet since 1995.
   b. I've been doing the Internet since 1995.
2. a. I've been baking for years.
   b. I've been breaking them for years.
3. a. She's been cleaning the animals.
   b. She's been feeding the animals.
4. a. He's been repairing them for more than five years.
   b. He's been preparing them for more than five years.
5. a. They've been living there for a year.
   b. They've been leaving there for a year.
6. a. You've been walking for an hour.
   b. You've been talking for an hour.

C. What's the Line?

Complete the conversations.

1. A. Do they make copies in Shipping?
   B. Yes. They've been making copies for two months.

2. A. Is Rita writing her monthly report?
   B. Yes. _____ it for the past two hours.

3. A. Can you operate a conveyor belt?
   B. Yes. _____ one since I started working here.

4. A. Can you and your brother repair cars?
   B. Yes. _____ them since we were teenagers.

5. A. Is Frank still fixing the copy machine?
   B. Yes. _____ it since 7:30 this morning.

6. A. Can you cook and bake?
   B. Yes. _____ since I moved away from home.

D. Open Road!

Tell about yourself.

I've been living in ..... (for since) .....

I've been studying English at ..... (for since) .....

I've been working at ..... (for since) .....

I've been ..... (for since) .....

I've been ..... (for since) .....

Tell About Job Responsibilities

Student Text
Pages 88-89

A. Wrong Way!

Put the lines in the correct order.

___ Certainly. What would you like to know?

___ Well, the zookeeper's primary responsibility is to oversee the employees and the animals.

___ Definitely! In my present job, I've been overseeing the animals and employees for years. And I wrote advertisements in the job I had before that.

_1_ Can you tell me anything more about the position?

___ In addition, the zookeeper writes advertisements for the zoo. Do you think you could handle those responsibilities?

___ I see.

___ What exactly are the zookeeper's responsibilities?

B. Listen

Listen to each person's work history, and put a check next to the correct information.

1. _✔_ He's been doing tune-ups.
   ___ He changes tires.
   _✔_ He changed tires before.

2. ___ She's been selling furniture.
   ___ She sells refrigerators.
   ___ She sold dishwashers before.

3. ___ He's been writing news stories.
   ___ He writes obituaries.
   ___ He wrote news stories before.

4. ___ She's been taking inventory.
   ___ She's been driving the van.
   ___ She drove the van before.

C. Open Road!

What responsibilities have you had in your jobs?

1. In my present job, I've been .....
2. In the job I had before that, I .....

Analyze Successful Job Interview Strategies

Student Text Pages 90-91

A. Good Advice or Bad Advice?

Decide if each of the following is good advice or bad advice for someone going to a job interview.

	Good Advice	*Bad Advice*
1 "Dress cleanly and neatly."	✓	
2 "Bring a copy of your resume."		
3 "Don't shake hands with the employer."		
4 "Be punctual."		
5 "Don't be polite."		
6 "Wait for the employer to invite you to sit down."		
7 "Don't look directly into the eyes of the interviewer."		
8 "Chew gum during the interview."		
9 "Don't prepare a list of questions about the job."		
10 "Be ready to answer questions about previous jobs."		
11 "Don't answer difficult questions."		
12 "Talk confidently about previous work experience."		
13 "Don't be truthful about your skills and abilities."		
14 "Say thank you for the time the person has spent with you."		

B. Listen

Listen to the interviews. What did each job applicant do wrong?

1. a. Mr. Smally didn't dress appropriately for the interview.
   (b.) Mr. Smally wasn't prepared to answer questions about his previous work experience.
   c. Mr. Smally didn't smile at the interviewer.

2. a. Ms. Short wasn't honest.
   b. Ms. Short wasn't capable and well-prepared.
   c. Ms. Short wasn't punctual.

3. a. Mr. Curtis didn't bring his resume to the interview.
   b. Mr. Curtis brought his family to the interview.
   c. Mr. Curtis wasn't honest with the interviewer.

4. a. Ms. Jackson wasn't on time.
   b. Ms. Jackson wasn't confident and truthful.
   c. Ms. Jackson asked inappropriate questions.

C. What's the Question?

What are the interviewer's questions?

1. A. Where have you worked before?
   B. I've worked at the Spandex Company and the Ajax Corporation.
2. A. .....?
   B. I worked at the Ajax Corporation from 1990 to 1995.
3. A. .....?
   B. My responsibilities? I typed reports and did the payroll.
4. A. .....?
   B. No, I don't work now. I'm a student.
5. A. .....?
   B. I've been a student since last September.
6. A. .....?
   B. I've been studying accounting and finance.
7. A. .....?
   B. I'll finish school next month.
8. A. .....?
   B. Yes. I have some questions about the company.

D. Fill It In!

Fill in the correct answer.

1. Job interviews are ____.
   (a.) critical
   b. capable
2. I have a very important ____.
   a. resume
   b. position
3. What ____ do you do in your job?
   a. exactly
   b. certainly
4. It's important to make a good ____.
   a. interview
   b. impression
5. Many ____ apply for the same position.
   a. applicants
   b. employers
6. My son has a new job with a lot of ____.
   a. experience
   b. responsibilities

Exit 6

Report an Emergency

Student Text Pages 94-95

A. Matching Lines

Match the lines.

d	1 My father has just fallen down a flight of stairs.	a. We'll send a squad car right away.
___	2 Someone has just broken into my house.	b. We'll send a repairperson right away.
___	3 A fire has just broken out in my house.	c. We'll send an animal removal specialist right away.
___	4 My hot water heater has just flooded my basement.	d. We'll send an ambulance right away.
___	5 A squirrel has just crawled into my house through the chimney.	e. We'll send an engine unit right away.

B. Listen

Listen and choose the next line of the conversation.

1. (a.) Could you send a repairperson right now?
   b. Could you send a medical specialist right away?
2. a. Call the carpenter!
   b. Call the ambulance service!
3. a. Call the fire department!
   b. Call the electrician!
4. a. Can you send an animal removal team right now?
   b. Can you send a police squad car right away?
5. a. Call the ASPCA right now!
   b. Call the heating company right now!
6. a. Call the police emergency unit!
   b. Call the ASPCA right away!

C. Open Road!

Report an emergency. What do you say?

A. .....

B. There's been an emergency!

A. .....

B. .....

A. .....

Report an Accident

Student Text
Pages 96-97

A. The Right Choice

Circle the correct word.

A. Police.

B. I want to (report tell)[1] an accident.

A. Yes. (Get Go)[2] ahead.

B. A truck has (overtuned overturned).[3]

A. What's your name?

B. Marilyn Jones.

A. (When Where)[4] did the accident (overturned happen)[5]?

B. (At On)[6] the expressway (near close)[7] Exit 45.

A. Did you (say tell)[8] Exit 49?

B. No, Exit 45.

A. All (okay right).[9] We'll (is be)[10] there right away.

B. What's the Word?

Complete each sentence with the correct form of the verb.

run over	fall through	break out	break into	fall down
rob	overturn	mug	land	crawl

1. Two people have just ___robbed___ a jewelry store on Main Street!
2. A helicopter has just _____ in the mall parking lot!
3. My grandmother has _____ the stairs!
4. Someone has just _____ my apartment!
5. A large truck has just _____ on the expressway!
6. A fire has _____ in my neighbor's house!
7. A skunk has _____ into my basement through a window!
8. An elderly couple has been _____ in front of the church!
9. Two children have been _____ by a car at 1600 Riverside Avenue!
10. Two workmen have _____ the roof of a house on Madison Avenue!

Ask for Recommendations in a Drug Store

Student Text
Pages 98-99

A. What's the Response?

Choose the correct response.

1. *Can you recommend something for a bad headache?*
   a. *I'd recommend nasal spray.*
   (b.) *I'd recommend aspirin tablets.*
2. *Can you suggest something for frizzy hair?*
   a. *Try hair spray.*
   b. *Try skin lotion.*
3. *What do you recommend for a stuffy nose?*
   a. *I suggest nasal spray.*
   b. *I suggest a cold.*
4. *Can you suggest something for dry skin?*
   a. *I'd suggest dry weather.*
   b. *I suggest dry skin lotion.*
5. *Can you recommend something for itchy, watery eyes?*
   a. *Try eyedrops.*
   b. *Try cold tablets.*
6. *What do you recommend for a bad backache?*
   a. *I'd suggest rest.*
   b. *I'd suggest freezing weather.*

B. Listen

Listen and choose the correct answer.

1. (a.) This person has a cold.
   b. This person has an earache.
2. a. This person is at home.
   b. This person is in a drug store.
3. a. The medicine is in Aisle D.
   b. The medicine is in Aisle C.
4. a. This person has a bad cold.
   b. This person has a backache.
5. a. Eyedrops are on the middle shelf.
   b. Eyedrops are on the bottom shelf.
6. a. This medicine is on the first shelf.
   b. This medicine is on the third shelf.
7. a. This person is looking for eyedrops.
   b. This person has a headache.
8. a. Hair spray is in the back of the store.
   b. Hair spray is in the front of the store.

Describe Symptoms and Make a Doctor's Appointment

Student Text Pages 100-101

A. What's the Response?

Choose the correct response.

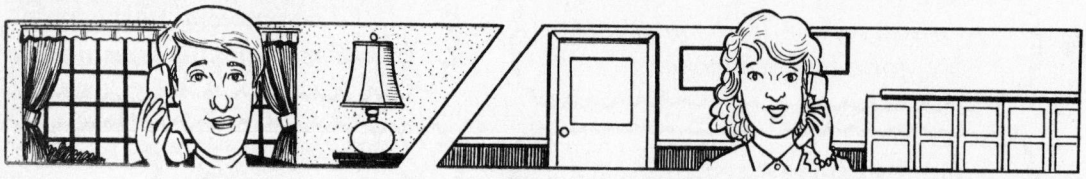

1. Hello. This is Paul Perkins calling.
   a. Doctor's office.
   (b.) What can I do for you?

2. I'm not feeling very well.
   a. What am I feeling?
   b. What's the problem?

3. What seems to be wrong?
   a. I feel dizzy and nauseous.
   b. I think I'm right.

4. I can't move my arm.
   a. I see.
   b. I'm sure.

5. How long have you been dizzy?
   a. Since three days.
   b. For three days.

6. Would you like to make an appointment?
   a. I want to make an appointment.
   b. Yes, please.

7. Is 3:00 tomorrow afternoon convenient?
   a. 3:00 tomorrow afternoon?
   b. Are you sure?

8. That's fine. Thank you very much.
   a. Okay. See you tomorrow.
   b. I haven't been feeling very well.

B. What's the Word?

Complete the sentences.

aren't	haven't	has	since
isn't	hasn't	had	for

1. My dog ___has___ been refusing to eat _____ three days.
2. My husband _____ had a terrible toothache for the past week.
3. I'm sorry you _____ feeling well.
4. The doctor _____ in the office now.
5. I've _____ a migraine headache all day.
6. Everyone at work _____ been dizzy and nauseous today.
7. My friend's ear _____ been ringing _____ Saturday.
8. The students in my English class _____ been feeling well this week.
9. My cat Chester is sick. He _____ eaten his cat food _____ a week.

C. Crosswalk

headache	toothache	dizzy	nauseous	backache
sore throat	stuffy nose	cough	watery eyes	dry skin

D. Listen

Listen and choose the sentence to finish the conversation.

1. a. Call the dentist right away.
   b. Call the doctor's office right away.
2. a. Call the animal hospital.
   b. Why don't you call the pharmacist?
3. a. I suggest you tell the supervisor.
   b. I suggest you call the dentist.
4. a. Call the dentist right away.
   b. Call an ambulance right away.
5. a. Call the animal hospital.
   b. Call an eye and ear doctor.
6. a. Ask a pharmacist for some lotion.
   b. Ask a pharmacist for some tablets.
7. a. Call the emergency medical team.
   b. Call the animal hospital.
8. a. He needs to see an ambulance.
   b. He needs to see a doctor.
9. a. Let's call the highway patrol.
   b. Let's call a mechanic.
10. a. Call the heating company.
    b. Call the emergency medical team.

Ask About and Give a Medical History

Student Text Pages 102-103

A. The Right Choice

Circle the correct words.

A. Well, Ms. Kramer, I think you've [giving / given] [1] me almost all the information I need for your medical history. Just one or two more [medical histories / questions] [2], if that's okay.

B. [Confidently / Certainly] [3].

A. Do you [had / have] [4] back trouble?

B. No, I [don't / haven't] [5].

A. And have you [ever / never] [6] [have / had] [7] a bad reaction to any drugs?

B. No, I [didn't / haven't] [8].

A. All right, Ms. Kramer. Please take a seat. The doctor will [been / be] [9] with you in a few minutes.

B. What's the Question?

Write the questions.

1. A. Has your husband ever been hospitalized?
   B. No, my husband has never been hospitalized.

2. A. _____?
   B. Yes, I'm allergic to penicillin.

3. A. _____?
   B. No, my dog Rover has never been on a special diet.

4. A. _____?
   B. No, my mother doesn't have any objection to herbs or other natural remedies.

5. A. _____?
   B. No, I don't have any history of heart disease in my family.

6. A. _____?
   B. No, my daughter has never had surgery before.

7. A. _____?
   B. No, I've never had a toothache before.

8. A. _____?
   B. Okay. I'll answer one or two more questions.

C. Sense or Nonsense?

Do the following "make sense" or are they "nonsense"?

	Sense	*Nonsense*
1 "Doctors use many different remedies for diseases."	✓	
2 "I'm allergic to stuffy noses."		
3 "Mr. Fenn is in back trouble."		
4 "I'm allergic to several medicines."		
5 "What diseases do you take?"		
6 "We're going to make your medical history."		
7 "I'm on a special diet."		
8 "My wife has been hospitalized three times."		
9 "The doctor will take your seat in a few minutes."		

Receive a Doctor's Medical Advice

Student Text Pages 104-105

A. The Right Choice

Choose the correct answer.

1. I'm concerned about your blood pressure.
   a. I urge you to change your diet.
   b. I urge you to stop going to rock concerts.

   Do you have any suggestions that might help?
   c. You should eat more salty food.
   d. You should look for a cookbook that has low-fat recipes.

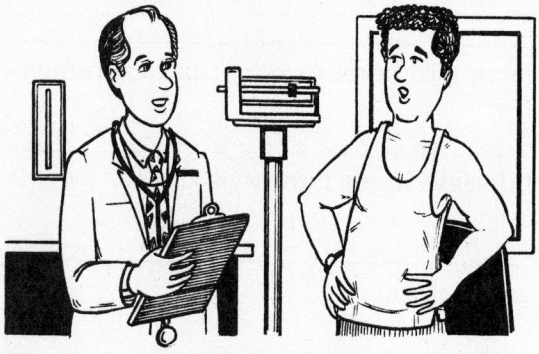

2. I'm concerned about your back.
   a. I urge you to join an organization to help you "kick the habit."
   b. I strongly advise you to begin a daily exercise routine.

   Do you have any suggestions that might help?
   c. You might join a yogurt class.
   d. You should do sit-ups every day.

3. I'm concerned about your hearing.
   a. I strongly advise you to change your eating habits.
   b. I urge you to change your music listening habits.

   Do you have any suggestions that might help?
   c. You might stop going to rock concerts.
   d. You should start going to rock concerts.

B. Listen

Listen and choose the sentence that is closest in meaning.

1. a. You've joined an organization to help you "kick the habit."
   b. You ought to join an organization to help you "kick the habit."

2. a. You have to cut back on your responsibilities.
   b. Your back is your responsibility.

3. a. You might change your eating habits.
   b. You need to change your eating habits.

4. a. I think you could find a hobby that you enjoy.
   b. You might have a good idea about that hobby.

5. a. It's necessary for you to begin an exercise routine.
   b. You've had an exercise routine.

6. a. You might eat less salty food.
   b. You must eat less salty food.

Receive a Pharmacist's Directions

Student Text Pages 106-109

A. Wrong Way!

Put the lines in the correct order.

___ I understand. Two pills after each meal.

___ Oh?

___ I see. Well, thanks very much.

_1_ Okay. Here's your prescription.

___ That's right. And one more thing. You could possibly feel dizzy after taking this medication.

___ Now be sure to follow the directions on the label. You need to take two pills after each meal.

___ Yes, but don't worry. That's a common side effect.

___ Thank you.

B. The 5th Wheel!

Which one doesn't belong?

1	You're supposed to	(You could possibly)	You've got to	You must
2	You may	It's possible that	You need to	You could possibly
3	It's essential	You could	You have to	You must
4	I suggest	Why don't you?	You have to	I'd recommend
5	You could	I urge you to	You might	It might be a good idea
6	What's the matter?	Can you suggest?	What's wrong?	What's the problem?
7	What was that?	What did you say?	What's that?	Can you recommend?

C. Listen

Listen and circle the word you hear.

1	(they)	they're	3	they're	their	5	they'll	they're
2	they'll	they've	4	their	they're	6	they'll	they've

D. What's the Ailment?

Read the solutions to common medical problems from student text page 108 and figure out the ailment.

sore throat	stomachache	cold	nose bleed	bee sting

1. "Pinch your nose." nose bleed
2. "Drink warm milk with honey, or lemon juice and honey." _____
3. "Take some antacids." _____
4. "Put a little vinegar on the skin." _____
5. "Have a bowl of homemade chicken soup." _____
6. "Drink some peppermint tea." _____
7. "Gargle with warm salty water." _____
8. "Tilt your head backward and rest it on the back of a chair." _____

E. WordRap: *My Doctor's Advice*

Listen. Then clap and practice.

You've got to be careful
What you eat.
Cut out sugar!
Cut down on meat!

Give up this!
Give up that!
Exercise!
And you won't get fat!

Take this medicine.
Do it right!
Take one in the morning
And two at night.

Read the directions
Carefully.
Take one at nine
And one at three.

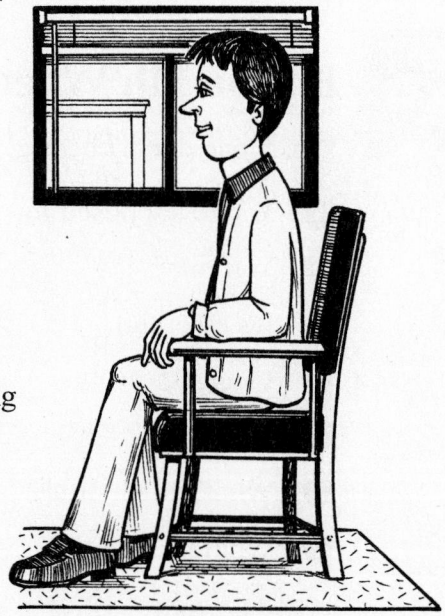

F. Open Road!

Tell about your favorite home remedy.

.....

.....

Offer Someone Medical Advice

Student Text Pages 110-111

A. Wrong Way!

Put the lines in the correct order.

___ Sure. What?

___ I have a bloody nose!

___ What's the problem?

_1_ Oh, no!

___ You ought to pinch your nose.

___ Well . . . You might tilt your head backward and rest it on the back of a chair.

___ Oh, that's too bad. Can I offer a suggestion?

___ Hmm. I'll give it a try. Thanks.

___ You know, I've tried pinching my nose when I've had a bloody nose before, and that doesn't work for me. Any other suggestions?

B. What's the Problem?

Decide what each person's problem is.

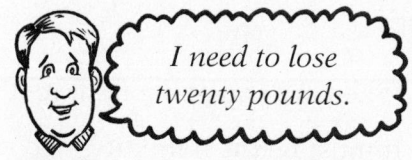

1 (a.) a weight problem
b. a hair problem

2 a. a stomachache
b. a sore shoulder

3 a. a fever
b. the hiccups

4 a. a backache
b. an earache

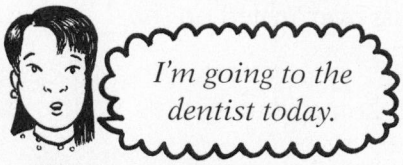

5 a. a toothache
b. a headache

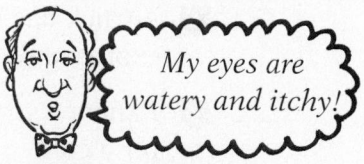

6 a. allergies
b. remedies

7 a. a cold
b. an earache

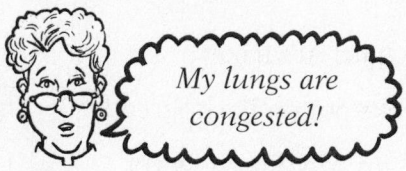

8 a. a toothache
b. the flu

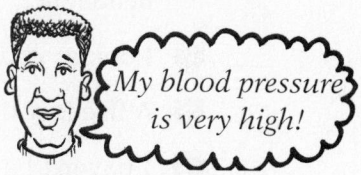

9 a. the hiccups
b. heart disease

Check-Up Test: Exits 4, 5, 6

A. The Right Choice

Circle the correct words.

1. We need a little / (a few) potatoes.
2. How many / much is the rent?
3. Please pick up a / some avocados.
4. Add a little / a few tomatoes to the stew.
5. Please get a / some six-pack of soda.
6. Try to get a gallon / a pound of chicken.
7. How much / many apples do you want?
8. Please buy a head / a bunch of cabbage.

B. Matching Lines

Match the lines.

e	1. You have to take these pills.	a. When are you going to have it?
___	2. I advise you to change your diet.	b. It must be the humidity.
___	3. You must stop smoking.	c. She should call her doctor.
___	4. A truck has just overturned on the expressway.	d. Drink hot water with lemon and honey.
___	5. I know a good home remedy for a cold.	e. Take them three times a day before meals.
___	6. Mary has a terrible migraine headache.	f. The highway patrol will be there right away.
___	7. Look at your hair! It's frizzy!	g. You ought to eat less salty food.
___	8. A fire just broke out on Park Street!	h. He has to do sit-ups every day.
___	9. I haven't had my job interview yet.	i. Call the fire department.
___	10. He's supposed to start exercising.	j. I'm concerned about your lungs.

C. Fill It In!

Fill in the correct answer.

1. _____ a delivery van.
   (a.) I've driven
   b. I'd driven

2. Has he _____ his promotion yet?
   a. got
   b. gotten

3. _____ in this building for a year.
   a. He's been leaving
   b. He's been living

4. I've already _____ the paychecks.
   a. given out
   b. gave out

5. _____ news stories every day.
   a. We've wrote
   b. We write

6. How long has she _____ type?
   a. is able to
   b. been able to

7. What _____ your responsibilities?
   a. are
   b. have

8. I haven't seen you _____ July.
   a. for
   b. since

9. It's _____ since Saturday.
   a. raining
   b. been raining

10. How long have you _____ them?
    a. known
    b. knew

11. Have you _____ used a computer?
    a. ever
    b. never

12. _____ have you been here?
    a. How long
    b. So long

13. _____ difficult to make?
    a. Have been
    b. Are they

14. _____ moussaka.
    a. I've never eaten
    b. I never eaten

15. _____ exercise next week.
    a. They'll
    b. They'd

16. _____ allergic to cats before.
    a. She's ever been
    b. She's never been

D. Listen

Listen and choose the best response.

1. a. I wasn't aware of that.
   (b.) Sure. I'd be happy to.
   c. Thanks a lot.

2. a. Can you sell computers?
   b. Now I've got it.
   c. Are you certain about that?

3. a. I'll say!
   b. What's new with you?
   c. You're supposed to.

4. a. You could make manicotti.
   b. I'm positive about that.
   c. Why don't you make pizza?

5. a. I'm sorry. I didn't realize that.
   b. I'm sure.
   c. Let me think.

6. a. You're welcome.
   b. Yes. I'm positive.
   c. Can I ask you a question?

7. a. That's too bad.
   b. I recommend that.
   c. That's right.

8. a. What's happening?
   b. You might try yoga.
   c. Who told you that?

Exit 7

Locate Items in a Department Store

Student Text Pages 116-117

A. Wrong Way!

Put the lines in the correct order.

___ Certainly. Take the escalator down two floors.

___ Stereos? They're in the Home Entertainment Department on the ground level.

___ Thank you very much.

1 Pardon me. Where are stereos located?

___ On the ground level? I see. Can you tell me how to get there?

B. Matching Lines

Match the items and departments.

e 1 beds

___ 2 microwave ovens

___ 3 pots and pans

___ 4 kids' jeans

___ 5 neckties

___ 6 dresses

___ 7 CD players

___ 8 returns

C. Listen

Listen and put a check next to the sentence you hear.

1 ✔ Dishwashers are on "9."

___ Dishwashers are fine.

2 ___ Returns are near the rear door.

___ Returns are at the rear of the store.

3 ___ Gloves are near the right entrance.

___ Gloves are near the side entrance.

4 ___ Women's shoes are in Aisle G.

___ Women's shoes are in Aisle 3.

D. What Am I?

Which department store item is "speaking"?

headphones	pastry	dishes	necktie	videocassette recorder
stove	television	coat	shoes	designer dress

1. "I'll be very important to you when you go outside next winter." coat
2. "If you rent a movie, I'll play it." _____
3. "You wear me on your feet every day." _____
4. "Come to the snack bar and enjoy me!" _____
5. "I'll cook dinner for you tonight." _____
6. "Mr. Miller will need me for his job interview." _____
7. "Turn me on and watch your favorite programs!" _____
8. "I hope you wash me after every meal!" _____
9. "Wear me to a friend's wedding!" _____
10. "If you don't want to have hearing problems, you should cut down on my use." _____

E. Fill It In!

Fill in the correct answer.

1. Dinner dishes are in the ____.
   a. side door
   (b.) basement
2. Where can I find ____?
   a. kitchen sets
   b. floors
3. Can you tell me ____?
   a. how to get there
   b. the first level
4. You can find lamps ____.
   a. in the side door
   b. near the side door
5. Women's blouses are on the ____.
   a. fourth floor
   b. rear
6. Go to ____ to return that.
   a. Custom Service
   b. Customer Service
7. ____ the escalator over there.
   a. Make
   b. Take
8. Could you tell me ____ the elevator is?
   a. where
   b. how
9. Walk up this staircase one ____.
   a. building
   b. flight
10. The elevator is on the ____.
    a. right in the corner
    b. corner in the right
11. Stereos? They're near the ____.
    a. floor
    b. rear door
12. Where are the TVs ____?
    a. located
    b. locate

Select Items in a Department Store

Student Text Pages 118-119

A. The Right Choice

Circle the correct words.

A. Do / May [1] I help you?

B. Yes. I want to buy / buy [2] a Casio watch.

A. Hmm. We carry Casio watches in several different modes / models [3].

B. I'd like the ones / one [4] that's also a calculator.

A. Okay. Let me see if that's / that [5] in stock. I'll be right back.

B. Sense or Nonsense?

Do the following "make sense" or are they "nonsense"?

		Sense	*Nonsense*
1	"This ice maker has a 19-inch screen."		✓
2	"This computer has 8 megabytes of memory."		
3	"I bought a vacuum cleaner that's also a calculator."		
4	"This color TV has a 13-inch screen and a remote control."		
5	"This refrigerator has a self-cleaning oven."		
6	"This microwave beeps when the food is ready."		
7	"You should definitely get the waterproof coffeemaker."		
8	"I recommend that you buy a refrigerator with remote control."		

C. Listen

Listen and circle the product the customer wants to buy.

1	gas range	TV	4	computer	TV
2	watch	refrigerator	5	coffeemaker	gas range
3	coffeemaker	computer	6	watch	refrigerator

D. Crosswalk

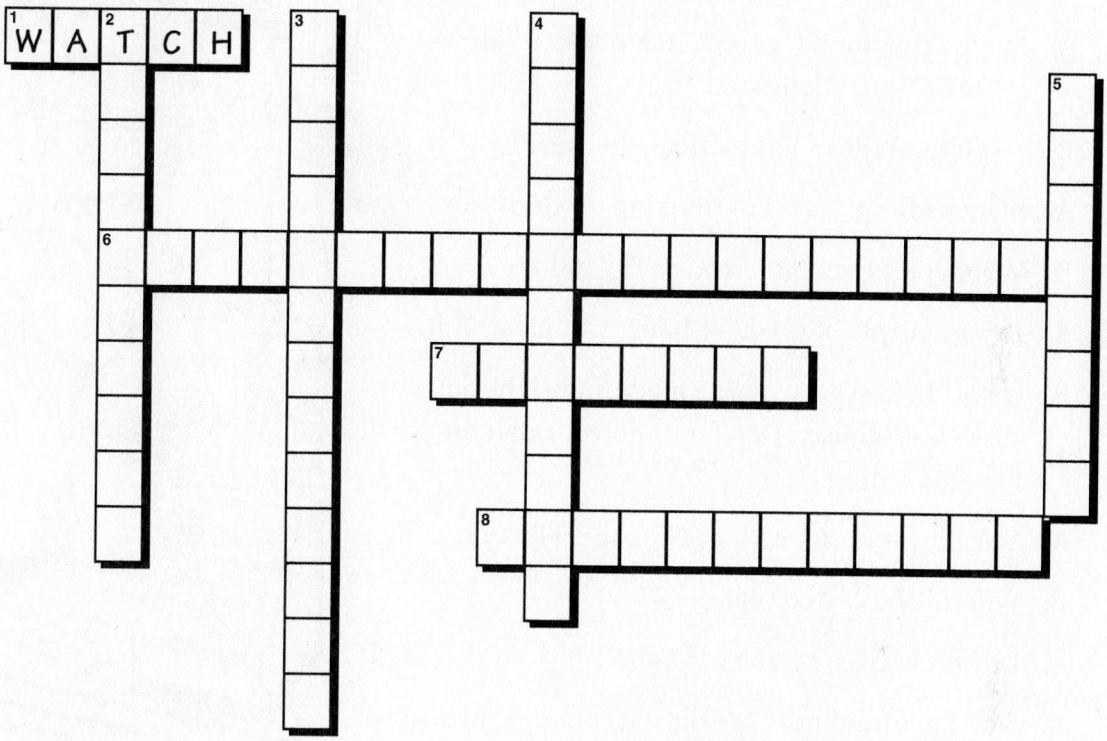

ACROSS

1. Is this one waterproof?
6. They're interested in one with remote control.
7. Does he have a personal one at home?
8. I want one with an automatic ice maker.

DOWN

2. Let me look at the one with a 27-inch screen.
3. This one beeps when the food is ready.
4. I need one that makes 12 cups.
5. We want one with a self-cleaning oven.

E. Open Road!

Recommend a product to a friend.

When you buy a ....., you should buy one with

.....

Purchase Items in a Department Store

Student Text Pages 120-121

A. The Right Choice

Circle the correct words.

A. Pardon me. (When (Could))[1] you help me?

B. (I'd be I've be)[2] happy to. What can I (make do)[3] for you?

A. I'm looking for a (press sleeveless)[4] blouse for my (son daughter)[5].

B. (What Whose)[6] size does she wear?

A. Size medium . . . (I'm thinking I think)[7].

B. What color (could would)[8] you like?

A. Bright purple, if (you've had you have)[9] it.

B. Okay. Let's see . . . a size medium bright purple sleeveless blouse. Do you think your daughter will like this (ones one)[10]?

A. Yes. I'm sure she will. (I'd take I'll take)[11] it.

B. Will this be cash or charge?

A. Do you (take make)[12] VISA?

B. No. I'm afraid not. We only accept our own store credit (cash card)[13].

A. Oh. In that case, I'll pay (credit card cash)[14].

B. Matching Lines

Match the description and the item.

e	1 I'd like size 7 black ____.	a. TV
___	2 I'm looking for a permanent press dress ____.	b. coffeemaker
___	3 Do you have a 25-inch color ____?	c. belt
___	4 I'm looking for a size 38 brown leather ____.	d. blouse
___	5 I'd like a small light green sleeveless ____.	e. sneakers
___	6 Do you have a beige 8-cup ____?	f. watch
___	7 I'm looking for a waterproof ____.	g. shirt

C. Wrong Way!

Put the words in the correct order.

1. a jogging red, white, and blue suit — a red, white, and blue jogging suit
2. a self-cleaning range gas _____
3. an machine washing automatic _____
4. jeans designer light blue _____
5. a waterproof brown dark watch _____
6. size 7 sneakers white _____
7. a shirt light blue press permanent _____
8. a leather large belt _____
9. an Computer Personal IBM _____
10. a yellow small purse plastic _____
11. permanent press beige pants _____
12. a dark green sleeveless medium blouse _____

D. Listen

Listen and choose the best response.

1. (a.) How large is the screen?
   b. Is it a black-and-white TV?
2. a. Is it for your living room?
   b. Where did you get it?
3. a. Do they have a V-neck?
   b. Are they designer jeans?
4. a. Is it a size 36?
   b. Is it leather or plastic?
5. a. I recommend one with a manual transmission.
   b. I recommend one with no transmission.
6. a. What size do you wear?
   b. What color does he like?
7. a. You should buy a 12-cup one.
   b. You should buy a leather one.
8. a. Is it automatic?
   b. Does it have a V-neck?
9. a. General Electric makes good ranges.
   b. Do you want one that beeps?
10. a. You should definitely get one with leather belts.
    b. You should get one with leather upholstery.

Return Items to a Department Store

Student Text Pages 122-125

A. The Right Choice

Circle the correct words.

A. (I'd want to (I want to))[1] return these earrings.

B. All right. Do you have the (recipe receipt)[2]?

A. Yes. Here you are.

B. (Would Could)[3] I ask why you're returning (them it)[4]?

A. Yes. (Their They're)[5] (to too)[6] large.

B. Would you like to (rechange exchange)[7] (it them)[8] for smaller (ones one)[9]?

A. No, I don't think so. (I I'd)[10] just like a (refund return)[11], please.

B. Certainly.

B. What's the Word?

1 *jeans:*	difficult	powerful	(tight)	young
2 *sofa:*	easy	comfortable	V-neck	automatic
3 *shirt:*	permanent press	plastic	8-cup	easy
4 *merchandise:*	powerful	in stock	tall	automatic
5 *prices:*	lightweight	sleeveless	bright	low
6 *VCR:*	expensive	conservative	tight	tall

C. WordRap: *Shopping Problems!*

Listen. Then clap and practice.

This suit doesn't fit.
Everything's wrong!
The sleeves are too short,
And the pants are too long!
It's not my size.
The jacket's too tight!
It's not my style,
And the color's not right!

These shoes are too small!
They look like a seven.
They aren't my size.
I need an eleven!
These gloves are too short,
And the color's all wrong!
I need a large size.
My fingers are long!

D. What's the Word?

Complete the following with the correct form of the adjective.

lightweight	fancy	big	short
powerful	easy	cheap	tight

1. This walkie-talkie set is too weak. I want one that's *more powerful*.

2. These pajamas are too long. I need a _____ pair.

3. This briefcase is too heavy. I want one that's _____.

4. These jeans are too large. I'd like to try a _____ pair.

5. I'd like to exchange this dress for one that's _____. This one is too conservative.

6. I'd like to exchange these shoes for ones that are _____. These are too expensive.

7. This computer game is too difficult. I want one that's _____.

8. This vest is too small. I'd like to try a _____ one.

E. Listen

Listen and choose the best response.

1. a. Those are more lightweight.
   b. The ones over there are lighter.
2. a. That one is simpler.
   b. That one is more powerful.
3. a. I'll try to find a darker one.
   b. I'll try to find a fancier one.
4. a. Let's look for a lighter one.
   b. Let's look for a smaller one.
5. a. I'm sure we can find a larger one.
   b. I'm sure we can find a tighter one.
6. a. Let's look for a shorter one.
   b. Let's look for a more powerful one.
7. a. Certainly. Is this one too long?
   b. Certainly. Is this one too tall?
8. a. The prices at Value World are lower.
   b. The prices at Value World are simpler.

Access the Services of a Post Office

Student Text Pages 126-129

A. Fill It In!

Fill in the correct answer.

1. I'd like to ____ this package.
   a. apply for
   (b.) mail
2. Sorry. You've got the ____ window.
   a. wrong
   b. right
3. I'd like to ____ a registered letter.
   a. send
   b. buy
4. Yes, you're at the ____ window.
   a. wrong
   b. right
5. Money orders can be ____ at the next window.
   a. purchased
   b. filed
6. Your mail is at the ____.
   a. box
   b. post office
7. I want to apply for ____.
   a. some packages
   b. a post office box
8. Stamps can be ____ at Window 2.
   a. bought
   b. mailed
9. I'd like to purchase a ____.
   a. change of address form
   b. money order
10. Aerogrammes can be ____ at Window 3.
    a. gotten
    b. got

B. Listen

Listen and choose the correct answer.

Conversation 1

1. a. The package is going to Boston.
   (b.) The package is going to Houston.
2. a. The package weighs seven pounds.
   b. The package weighs eleven pounds.
3. a. First class is $8.75.
   b. Parcel post is $8.75.
4. a. The customer decides to send the package parcel post.
   b. The customer decides to send the package first class.

Conversation 2

5. a. The package is going to Miami.
   b. The package is going to Naomi.
6. a. It's cheaper to send it parcel post.
   b. It's cheaper to send it first class.
7. a. Parcel post is faster.
   b. First class is faster.
8. a. The customer decides to send the package parcel post.
   b. The customer decides to send the package first class.

C. Matching Lines

Match the questions and answers.

d	1 How would you like to send this package?	a. Yes. That's what it'll cost to send it first class.
___	2 How much does it weigh?	b. It has to be there by this Friday.
___	3 Eighteen dollars and forty cents?	c. Eighteen dollars and forty cents.
___	4 How much do I owe you?	d. First class, please.
___	5 Will it take longer by parcel post?	e. Yes. It'll take ten days to get there.
___	6 When do you need it to get there?	f. Yes. Parcel post would be ten dollars.
___	7 Is it cheaper to send it parcel post?	g. Seventeen pounds.

D. More Matching Lines

Match the words.

c	1 bowling	a. gift	___	4 unabridged	d. oven
___	2 wedding	b. bowl	___	5 electric	e. dictionary
___	3 crystal punch	c. ball	___	6 toaster	f. toaster

E. Open Road!

You're sending a package. Complete the conversation any way you wish.

A. I'd like to mail this package to ..... .

B. How would you like to send it?

A. First class, please.

B. Okay. Let me see. It's ..... pounds, so that'll be $..... .

A. $.....?

B. Yes. That's a pretty heavy package you've got there.

A. I guess it is. It's (a/an) ..... I'm sending to ..... . How long will it take to get there?

B. About ..... days.

A. About ..... days? That's fine.

Discuss Features of Products

Student Text Pages 130-131

A. What's the Word?

Complete the conversation.

feature	passengers	decision	trips	controls
finest	stereo	particular	CD	installment
write up	point out	reclines	shop around	spread out

A. May I help you?

B. Yes. I'm interested in this car.

A. You have very good taste. This is one of the ___finest___ [1] cars we have.

B. Really?

A. Yes. Let me _____ [2] some of its special features.

B. Okay.

A. First, notice that the _____ [3] on the dashboard are all computerized.

B. Hmm. I see that.

A. Also, the seat fully _____ [4] so that your _____ [5] can sleep during those long _____ [6].

B. That's a very nice _____ [7].

A. I should also point out that an AM-FM _____ [8] radio with _____ [9] player is included.

B. Oh. That's very interesting. Can I ask how much it costs?

A. Of course. This _____ [10] car costs $20,000, and let me mention that we offer a very good _____ [11] plan to help you _____ [12] the payments.

B. I see.

A. Would you like me to _____ [13] an order slip for you?

B. Not right now, thanks. I want to _____ [14] a little more before I make a _____ [15].

Exit 8

Make Plans

Student Text Pages 134-135

A. The Right Choice

Circle the correct words.

A. What do you want to [1] doing / (do) today?

B. I don't know. Do you have any suggestions?

A. What about [2] hang out / hanging out at the shopping mall?

B. Hmm. I'm not really in the mood to [3] hang out / hanging out at the shopping mall. Any other ideas?

A. Well, what about [4] playing / play basketball?

B. Good idea! We haven't [5] play / played basketball in a long time.

B. Listen

Listen and put a check next to what these people are going to do today.

1. ___ They're going to see a movie.
   ✔ They're going to go jogging.

2. ___ They're going to go bowling.
   ___ They're going to have a picnic.

3. ___ They're going to play tennis.
   ___ They're going to go to the ballgame.

4. ___ They're going to go fishing.
   ___ They're going to go swimming.

Discuss Recreation Preferences

Student Text Pages 136-137

A. Wrong Way!

Put the lines in the correct order.

___ I think I'd prefer to go to the Art Museum.

___ Good idea. Which one do you want to go to?

_1_ Why don't we go to a museum today?

___ I don't care. Which one would you rather go to?

___ Okay. That's fine with me.

___ Oh, I don't know. How about going to the Art Museum? Or we could always go the Museum of Natural History.

B. Matching Lines

Match the expressions that have the same meaning.

_e_	1 Let's . . .	a. I'd prefer to . . .
___	2 I'd rather . . .	b. I don't really feel like . . .
___	3 It doesn't matter to me.	c. How about . . . ?
___	4 What about . . . ?	d. Good suggestion!
___	5 I'm not really in the mood to . . .	e. Why don't we . . . ?
___	6 Good idea!	f. It doesn't make any difference to me.

C. Open Road!

Complete the conversation any way you wish.

A. Let's ..... today!

B. Good idea! (What/Where) .....?

A. Oh, I don't know. How about .....?

Or we could .....

B. It doesn't matter to me. What would you rather do?

A. I think I'd rather .....

B. Okay. That's fine with me.

D. Listen

Listen and circle what these people are going to do today.

1. ride their bikes / (take a hike)
2. go bowling / stay home
3. watch TV / go to the movies
4. play hopscotch / play "hide and seek "
5. visit a museum / see a film
6. go skating / have a picnic

E. What's the Line?

Complete the conversations with the correct verb forms.

play/playing	see/seeing	ride/riding	take/taking	swim/swimming
have/having	go/going	visit/visiting	do/doing	drive/driving

1. Do you feel like driving to the beach?
   I think I'd prefer to ride our bikes.

2. What do you want to _____ today?
   How about _____ the new Disney film?

3. Do you have any suggestions?
   Yes. Let's _____ hopscotch.
   I'd rather _____ "hide and seek."

4. How about _____ the kids to the zoo? Or we could _____ a picnic.
   Anything is fine with me.

5. Let's go _____ today!
   Good idea. Where do you want to go?
   It doesn't make any difference to me. How about _____ to the town pool?

6. Which museum do you want to go to?
   How about _____ the Art Museum?
   I'd rather _____ to the Basketball Museum.

Extend Invitations

Student Text Pages 138-139

A. The Right Choice

Circle the correct words.

A. Would you be interested in ((taking) take)[1] a ride in the country tomorrow?

B. (I love to I'd love to)[2]. I (have taken haven't taken)[3] a ride in the country in a long time. But wait a minute. Isn't it (suppose to supposed to)[4] snow tomorrow?

A. Gee. (I hadn't heard I don't hear)[5] that.

B. I'm pretty sure it's going to snow. They (told said)[6] so on TV.

A. In that case, (taking take)[7] a ride probably (would wouldn't)[8] be a good idea.

B. Hmm. I guess (you're your)[9] right.

A. Let's wait and see what the weather (be is)[10] like tomorrow.

B. Okay. I'll call you in the morning.

B. Sense or Nonsense?

Do the following "make sense" or are they "nonsense"?

	Sense	*Nonsense*
1 "I heard it on the morning news."	✓	
2 "I read it in the paper."		
3 "I watched it on the radio."		
4 "The weather forecaster on TV predicted it."		
5 "It rained on the morning news."		

C. Listen

Listen and choose the best activity based on the weather.

1. a. Playing tennis is a good idea.
   (b.) Going bowling is a good idea.
2. a. Playing golf sounds like fun.
   b. Going skating sounds like fun.
3. a. Going skiing would be fun.
   b. Seeing a movie would be fun.
4. a. Going sailing is a good idea.
   b. Going sailing isn't a good idea.
5. a. Staying home sounds great.
   b. Driving around the city sounds great.
6. a. Playing football is a good suggestion.
   b. Going to the beach is a good idea.

Decline Invitations

Student Text Pages 140-141

A. What's the Meaning?

Choose the answer that is the closest in meaning.

1. "Would you by any chance be interested in going to a concert this weekend?"
   a. Do you have to go to a concert this weekend?
   b Would you prefer to go to a concert this weekend?
   (c.) Do you want to go to a concert this weekend?

2. "I'm afraid I won't be able to go. I have to take care of my friend's children."
   a. I can't go because I've got to do something else.
   b. My friend's children won't be able to go.
   c. I'm afraid I won't be able to take care of my friend's children.

3. "Going out for dinner sounds like more fun than attending a business meeting."
   a. Attending business meetings is better than going out for dinner.
   b. I'd rather go out for dinner than attend a business meeting.
   c. I recommend going to business meetings.

B. The Right Choice

Which activities belong in each of these categories?

1. **Indoor Recreation**
   - ___ driving to the beach
   - ✔ seeing a play
   - ✔ going to a museum
   - ___ playing golf

2. **Water Activities**
   - ___ having a picnic
   - ___ roller skating
   - ___ swimming
   - ___ fishing

3. **Games You Play with a Ball**
   - ___ soccer
   - ___ tennis
   - ___ hockey
   - ___ basketball

4. **Outdoor Recreation**
   - ___ seeing a play
   - ___ taking a hike
   - ___ going to a concert
   - ___ riding a bike

5. **Children's Activities**
   - ___ playing hopscotch
   - ___ playing "hide and seek"
   - ___ playing golf
   - ___ riding a bike

6. **Work Responsibilities**
   - ___ hanging out at the mall
   - ___ attending a meeting
   - ___ writing a report
   - ___ visiting a friend

C. Accepted or Rejected?

Did the person accept or reject the invitation?

	Accept	Reject
1 "I'd really like to go skating at the rink."	✓	
2 "I'm sorry. I have to do my homework."		
3 "It's foggy, so sailing probably wouldn't be a good idea."		
4 "Hanging out at the shopping mall sounds like fun."		
5 "Watching a comedy sounds like a good idea."		
6 "I'm not in the mood to take a hike."		
7 "Maybe some other time."		
8 "Going on a picnic in the rain wouldn't be very enjoyable."		

D. WordRap: *Invitations*

Listen. Then clap and practice.

A. Would you like to come with us?
We're planning to ski.
B. Sorry. I can't.
I've got a bad knee.

A. Let's go swimming.
We'll try the new pool.
B. I'd love to join you,
But I'm leaving for school.

A. Would you like to go sailing?
The weather looks great.
B. I'm sorry. I can't.
I've got a big date!

A. Would you like to have dinner
With my Uncle Paul?
B. Sorry. I can't.
I'm expecting a call.

A. Let's make that new recipe.
I'm dying to try it.
B. I'd really like to,
But I'm still on my diet.

A. Would you like to watch Fido
Do a cute little trick?
B. Sorry. I can't.
I'm feeling sick.

Tell About Weekend Activities

Student Text Pages 142-143

A. The Right Choice

Circle the correct words.

A. What [1] (had you done / did you do) over the weekend?

B. I [2] (flew / had flown) my kite.

A. [3] (Did / Had) you [4] (enjoyed / enjoy) it?

B. Yes. I [5] (didn't fly / hadn't flown) my kite in ages! What [6] (did / had) YOU [7] (done / do)?

A. I [8] (had driven / drove) to the mountains.

B. Hmm. Didn't you drive to the mountains the weekend before?

A. Yes, I [9] (didn't / did). And I [10] (had driven / driven) there the weekend before THAT, too!

B. Boy, you really enjoy [11] (drive / driving) to the mountains!

A. I sure do! I [12] (liked / like) to drive to the mountains [13] (whatever / whenever) I can.

B. Fill It In!

Fill in the correct answer.

1. Dan didn't go to the mall last Sunday because ____.
   a. he had gone there on Friday
   b. he hadn't gone there on Friday

2. I enjoyed wearing a tuxedo to the wedding because ____.
   a. I had worn a tuxedo in ages
   b. I hadn't worn a tuxedo in ages

3. I washed my windows last week because ____.
   a. I hadn't washed them in ages
   b. I had washed them in ages

4. I decided to volunteer at my son's school because ____.
   a. I hadn't volunteered before
   b. I had volunteered before

5. Gary got into a motorcycle accident last week because ____.
   a. he had ridden in four years
   b. he hadn't ridden in four years

6. Susan rejected Bill's invitation to see the play because ____.
   a. she had already seen it
   b. she hadn't seen it

C. What's the Response?

Choose the correct response.

1. Did you see the ballgame on TV last night?
   a. Yes. I didn't see a ballgame in ages.
   b. Yes. I hadn't seen a ballgame in ages.

2. Is it true you read three novels last week?
   a. Yes. That's because I had had time to read a long time.
   b. Yes. That's because I hadn't had time to read in a long time.

3. Peter looked nauseous when I saw him yesterday afternoon.
   a. He had eaten too much candy for lunch.
   b. He hadn't eaten too much candy for lunch.

D. Listen

Listen and circle the word you hear.

1	wash	watch	6	done	gone	11	made	baked
2	written	ridden	7	seemed	seen	12	play	skate
3	hurt	heard	8	flown	known	13	drove	told
4	sent	send	9	hiked	biked	14	bought	got
5	said	read	10	wanted	gotten	15	done	drawn

Tell About Experiences

Student Text Pages 144-145

A. What Are They Saying?

Complete the conversation.

A. Did you know that my husband and I won the lottery last year?

B. You (*predict*) ___had been predicting___ [1] you would win for ages! That's fantastic!

A. I know, but I can't believe it finally happened.

B. What did you do with your lottery winnings?

A. First, my husband and I went to Antarctica. We (*think*) _____ [2] about going there for a long time.

B. Did you enjoy it?

A. It was incredible! We (*expect*) _____ [3] it to be exciting, but it was better than we had anticipated.

B. That's great. Tell me, what else did you do with your winnings?

A. We bought a new house. We (*want*) _____ [4] to buy one for years.

B. That's wonderful.

A. Oh, and I almost forgot to tell you. We took our children on a trip to South America. They (*hope*) _____ [5] to go to South America their whole lives.

B. Did you have a good time?

A. We had a wonderful trip!

B. Listen

Listen and decide what these people are talking about.

1. (a.) a cruise
   b. a bus trip
2. a. dinner at home
   b. dinner at a restaurant
3. a. a plane ride
   b. a train ride
4. a. a vacation
   b. a picnic
5. a. a trip to the beach
   b. a dance
6. a. a TV program
   b. a movie

Use the Newspaper to Make Movie Plans

Student Text Pages 146-147

A. What's the Response?

Choose the correct response.

1. Would you like to see a movie tonight?
   (a.) Sure.
   b. *The Cowboy Story.*
2. What would you like to see?
   a. What about a comedy?
   b. What's an adventure?
3. How about *A Journey into Space*?
   a. Do you want to see a movie?
   b. *A Journey into Space*?
4. What's it about?
   a. I don't know.
   b. I don't know it.
5. What did the ad in the paper say?
   a. It said, "It's beyond the universe!"
   b. It said it in the paper.
6. Is it a mystery?
   a. Yes. It's a documentary.
   b. No. It's a science fiction movie.
7. Who's in it?
   a. Barbara Burns and Dan Donner.
   b. A science fiction movie.
8. Are you interested?
   a. Sure. I'm interesting.
   b. Sure. I'm interested.
9. What time is it showing?
   a. There are shows at 7 and 9.
   b. It's at the City Cinema.
10. I'd rather go at 7.
    a. That's fine with me.
    b. That's fine to be.

B. Matching Lines

Match the lines.

d	1. City Cinema is proud to present ____.	a. 6:00 in the evening
___	2. The afternoon shows are at ____.	b. foreign film
___	3. Tickets are $3.00 before ____.	c. Fresh Pond Cinema
___	4. Evening tickets cost ____.	d. *The Berry Bears*
___	5. Thanks for calling ____.	e. $6.50
___	6. The shows this evening are at ____.	f. 1:15 and 3:45
___	7. *El Agua* is this week's special ____.	g. 7:15 and 9:45

C. Open Road!

Tell about your favorite kinds of movies.

.....

.....

.....

.....

D. Listen

Listen and choose the best name for the movie.

1. (a.) *Illnesses of the 21st Century*
   b. *The Great Space War*
2. a. *Lost Love*
   b. *Laugh Time*
3. a. *The Twin Dogs Meet Santa Claus*
   b. *Journey into Deep Space*
4. a. *The Search for the Missing Jewels*
   b. *The Berry Bears Adventure*
5. a. *Agua Caliente*
   b. *Cats and Dogs Everywhere*
6. a. *The French Countryside Today*
   b. *Cowboys on the Run*

E. Crosswalk

What kinds of movies?

1. *The Lost Island*
2. *Toys on Parade*
3. *Asia Today*
4. *Invaders from Mars*
5. *El Hombre*
6. *Good-bye Forever*
7. *Stories of the Old West*
8. *A Time to Laugh*
9. *Dilly Ducks Adventure*
10. *The Missing Watch*

Discuss Television Preferences

Student Text Pages 148-151

A. The Right Choice

Circle the correct word.

A. What do you want to (watch wash)[1]?

B. I don't know. What's (in on)[2]?

A. Well, *The Mystery Hour* (is it's)[3] on Channel 7.

B. Oh, I'd rather (not no)[4] watch *The Mystery Hour*. I'm tired of (watch watching)[5] that program. What else is on?

A. Well, (there's it's)[6] a new miniseries on Channel 6.

B. I'm not really in the (mood moon)[7] for a miniseries. (Do Are)[8] you?

A. No, I (guest guess)[9] not. How about (watch watching)[10] *The Game of Fortune* on Channel 12? That's supposed to be a pretty good game show.

B. *The Game of Fortune*? I don't know. Maybe we (must should)[11] watch *The Mystery Hour* after all.

A. It doesn't (difference matter)[12] to me.

B. Are you sure?

A. Yes. (Whenever Whatever)[13] you'd like to watch is fine with me.

B. Sense or Nonsense?

Do the following "make sense" or are they "nonsense"?

	Sense	*Nonsense*
1 "Going to the movies can be enjoyable."	✓	
2 "People have to stand in line to buy tickets at home."		
3 "A VCR offers an alternative to a night at the movies."		
4 "People can rent movies from their neighbors."		
5 "Watching a movie at home can be convenient."		
6 "VCRs cost about three dollars to buy."		
7 "Some people prefer to rent movies at movie theaters."		
8 "Popcorn is an example of modern technology."		

Check-Up Test: Exits 7, 8

A. The Right Choice

Circle the correct word.

1. These jeans are too tight. I 'd like to try a (smaller (larger)) pair.
2. This briefcase is too heavy. I'd like one that's more (lightweight powerful).
3. These earrings are too fancy. I'd like to exchange them for more (conservative difficult) ones.
4. The prices in this catalog are too high. I need to find a catalog with (lower smaller) prices.
5. Skiing is very expensive. I want to try a (cheaper larger) sport.
6. The weather here is too cold. I want to live where the weather is (colder warmer).

B. Matching Lines

Match the lines that have the same meaning.

d	1. May I help you?	a. Do you have any ideas?
___	2. Where can I find them?	b. I suppose.
___	3. Do you have any suggestions?	c. I'd rather do that.
___	4. I won't be able to.	d. Can I help you?
___	5. I'd prefer to do that.	e. It doesn't make any difference.
___	6. I'd like to do that.	f. That sounds like fun.
___	7. I guess.	g. Where are they located?
___	8. That sounds great!	h. I want to do that.
___	9. It doesn't matter to me.	i. I can't.

C. Wrong Way!

Put the words in the correct order.

1. a dress bright green — a bright green dress
2. a large sweater blue light — _____
3. a beige belt size 34 — _____
4. a shirt white press permanent — _____
5. a plastic light brown purse — _____

D. Listen

Listen and choose the correct answer.

1. (a.) find one with remote control
   b. getting one with a large screen
2. a. doing
   b. go
3. a. finding a skirt
   b. look for a blouse
4. a. going to a ballgame
   b. see a play
5. a. cook tonight
   b. washing my car
6. a. exchange them for a bigger pair
   b. returning them
7. a. visiting a museum
   b. go for a drive
8. a. go to the zoo
   b. playing tennis
9. a. work in my garden
   b. reading a novel
10. a. sail
    b. going out to dinner

E. What's the Line?

Complete the sentences.

1. I enjoyed the concert. I (*go*) hadn't gone to a concert in a long time.
2. I loved playing golf last week. I (*play*) _____ golf for several years.
3. I really enjoyed that movie. I (*see*) _____ a movie in ages.
4. We fell when we went roller skating because we (*go*) _____ roller skating in a long time.
5. Fred wore his new tie to work yesterday. He (*wear*) _____ it before.

F. What's the Line?

Complete the sentences.

1. I enjoyed my vacation. I (*plan*) had been planning it for a long time.
2. I was disappointed in the new restaurant. Everyone (*tell*) _____ me how good the food was.
3. The Senior Prom was boring. It's too bad. We (*look forward*) _____ to it all year.
4. We (*hope*) _____ for good weather for our party, and we were lucky! It was sunny and clear.
5. It's a shame you had a miserable vacation. You (*talk*) _____ about your plans for months.
6. I finally had to get a new radiator for my car last week. My old radiator (*leak*) _____ for weeks.

SCRIPTS FOR LISTENING EXERCISES

Page 1

Listen and circle the word you hear.

1. Which apartment do you live in?
2. Who is your supervisor?
3. What floor do you live on?
4. How did you meet them?
5. Whose class is this?
6. Why are you majoring in mathematics?

Page 3

Listen and decide what they're talking about.

1. Does it leave for downtown every fifteen minutes?
2. Who is your supervisor?
3. Whose class are you in?
4. How did you hurt yourself, Mrs. Martinez?
5. Which floor do you live on?
6. Which department do you work in?
7. How do you feel, Mr. Davis?
8. Does it stop in front of the building?
9. How do the neighbors like it here?

Page 4

Listen and choose the correct people.

1. I'd like to introduce my wife and my daughters.
2. These are my parents.
3. This is my nephew.
4. Let me introduce you to my brother and his wife.
5. These are my nieces.
6. I'd like to introduce my mother-in-law.

Page 6

Listen and circle the correct word.

1. When I'm in Florence, I speak . . . .
2. I'm going to Kyoto on vacation to practice my . . . .
3. I'm moving to Stockholm. That's why I'm learning . . . .
4. This is my friend Manuel. He's a . . . .
5. I love to drink Brazilian coffee. I drank it every day when I was in . . . .
6. Seoul is my favorite city in . . . .
7. On my next vacation I'm going to . . . .
8. The national language of Colombia is . . . .
9. In Montreal, people speak English and . . . .

Page 8

Listen and choose the correct response.

1. May I help you?
2. First name Thomas?
3. Are you traveling alone?
4. Are you paying by check?
5. I see here you requested a regular room.
6. How long do you plan to stay?
7. You asked for a room facing the park.
8. My name is George Williston.

Page 13

Listen and decide if it's "good news" or "bad news."

1. I didn't get a promotion!
2. I got a big raise!
3. I flunked my English exam!
4. My daughter graduated from high school last month!
5. Nobody remembered my birthday!
6. I found twenty dollars on the street on my way to work this morning!
7. I got a ticket for speeding today!
8. I left my keys in the house, and now I can't get in!
9. My husband wrecked our new car!
10. Someone took my wallet!

Page 17

Listen and write the number under the correct picture.

1. A. Did the Abro Corporation buy our company?
   B. No. Where did you hear that?
   A. I heard it in the cafeteria.
   B. Well, I can't believe it's true. I'm sure it's just a rumor.
2. A. Can I ask you a question?
   B. Sure. What?
   A. Are the people across the street getting a divorce?
   B. I don't know. Where did you hear that?
   A. All the neighbors are talking about it.
3. A. Are the bus drivers going on strike?
   B. I don't know. Where did you hear that?
   A. Someone mentioned it at the bus stop.
4. A. Did you know that they're going to lay off the workers on the night shift?
   B. Who told you that?
   A. I heard it from the security guard.
   B. Well, I can't believe it's true. I'm sure it's just a rumor.
5. A. Our supervisor wants to shorten our coffee break.
   B. Where did you hear that?
   A. One of the secretaries told me.
   B. Well, I can't believe it's true!
6. A. Did you know that our English teacher was in the 1996 Olympics?
   B. Where did you hear that?
   A. Someone in science class told me.
7. A. I hear that Mrs. Anderson canceled our class picnic.
   B. Really? Where did you hear that?
   A. I heard it in gym class.
   B. Well, I can't believe it's true. I'm sure it's just a rumor.
8. A. Did you know that Santa Claus is just "make believe"?
   B. Who told you that?
   A. One of the girls in my class told me.

Page 21

Listen and number the activities.

1. A. What are you and your husband going to do this weekend?
   B. On Friday evening, we're going to go dancing. On Saturday, we're going to clean out our attic. It's really a mess! And on Sunday, I think we'll go to the beach.
2. A. What are you going to do this weekend?
   B. I'm pretty sure I'll finish my term paper on Friday evening. On Saturday morning, I'll most likely go food shopping. And on Sunday, I'm going to play tennis.
3. A. What's Marge going to do at work today?
   B. First, she'll finish typing a letter for her boss. Then, she'll take a break. And then, she'll go to the post office to mail some packages.
4. A. What are your children going to do this weekend?
   B. They'll most likely go to the movies on Friday evening. On Saturday morning, they're going to clean their rooms. And on Saturday afternoon, I'm going to take them to the circus.

Page 22

Listen and choose the correct response.

1. So, tell me a little about yourself.
2. What do you want to know?
3. I'm originally from Seattle. How about you?
4. Do you still live in Cleveland?
5. Tell me about your family.

6. How about you? Do you have any brothers or sisters?
7. Tell me, what do you do?
8. How about you? What do YOU do?

Page 24

Listen and circle the word you hear.

1. On Friday nights, I like to relax after work.
2. I'm going to take my brother to the theater on Sunday.
3. We'll probably go to a play on Saturday.
4. I'll most likely do chores on Saturday afternoon.
5. Many people have brunch on Sunday.
6. When the weather is nice, I like to take my children to the zoo.
7. Our grandparents are going to visit this weekend.
8. What programs do you like to watch?
9. Do you want to go to a rock concert with me this Saturday evening?

Page 26

Listen and put a check next to the sentence you hear.

1. I hear about it every day.
2. Go to the corner and turn right.
3. I walk to the store every day.
4. Do you have any plans?
5. That telephone number is wrong!
6. She won't go to work tomorrow.
7. That teacher taught math.
8. Sally won the race.

Page 26

Listen and write the spelling of each name.

1. The name is Lawler: L-A-W-L-E-R.
2. The name is Ying: Y-I-N-G.
3. The name is Mills: M-I-L-L-S.
4. The name is Potsky: P-O-T-S-K-Y.
5. The name is Gomez: G-O-M-E-Z.
6. The name is Jarvis: J-A-R-V-I-S.

Page 32

Look at the map and listen to the directions. If the directions are correct, write C. If they are incorrect, write I.

1. A. Do you know how to get to the movie theater?
   B. Sure. Go up Main Street three blocks and turn right onto Second Avenue. Walk along Second Avenue, and you'll see the movie theater on the left, at the intersection of Second Avenue and Park Street.
   A. Thank you very much.
2. A. Excuse me. Is there a laundromat around here?
   B. Yes. There's a laundromat on Third Avenue. Go along Fifth Avenue two blocks. Turn left onto Center Street. Walk two blocks. You'll see the laundromat on the right, at the intersection of Center Street and Third Avenue.
   A. Thanks.
3. A. Excuse me. I'm looking for the bank. Can you help me?
   B. Sure. Follow Fifth Avenue to Middle Street. Turn right on Middle Street and walk two blocks. You'll see the bank across from City Hall.
   A. Thank you.
4. A. Excuse me. Where's the City Zoo?
   B. The zoo? Hmm. Let me see. Follow Fifth Avenue to Park Street. You'll see the zoo on your left, at the intersection of Park Street and Fifth Avenue.
   A. Thank you very much.
5. A. Is there a hospital nearby?
   B. Yes. Walk up Main Street two blocks. Take a left on Third Avenue. Follow Third Avenue to Middle Street. You'll see the hospital on your right.
   A. Thanks.
6. A. Excuse me. I'm looking for a supermarket. Can you help me?
   B. Sure. Walk along Fifth Avenue to Center Street. Turn left on Center Street and walk two blocks. You'll see the supermarket on the corner, across from the fire station.
   A. Thank you very much.
7. A. Pardon me. Is there a parking lot nearby?
   B. Yes. Go up Main Street one block. You'll see a parking lot on the right, near the police station.
   A. Thanks.
8. A. Could you possibly tell me how to get to the bus station?
   B. Uh-húh. The bus station is right over there, at the intersection of Middle Street and Fifth Avenue.
   A. Oh, thanks. I see it.
9. A. Pardon me. Do you know how to get to the library?
   B. Yes. Walk up Main Street two blocks. You'll see the library on your right, at the intersection of Main Street and Third Avenue.
   A. Thank you.

Page 36

Listen to the traffic report and choose the correct answers.

1. This is Ned Green, your TV 5 traffic reporter, with a rush hour traffic report. There's an accident on Highway 12 near Exit 15. The traffic is stopped. Commuters should take the subway to get to work.
2. Good morning, WCBY listeners. There's an accident on the subway this morning. The trains are very slow and crowded. Commuters should try to hail a cab to get to work.
3. This is the WSDK evening rush hour report. It's snowing, and the trains and buses are late. Getting home from work will be difficult tonight.
4. Today WRTD has some good news for commuters. The new subway system is open! Commuters can ride underground on comfortable new trains.

Page 37

Listen and circle the word you hear.

1. We went to Peru for our vacation.
2. My son-in-law wrecked my new car!
3. For directory assistance, dial 411.
4. Your directions were excellent. I found your house easily.
5. I overheard some people say the boss fired his secretary!
6. My husband left our son at school.
7. I'm sorry, but all of your flowers died!
8. I can't believe it's true!
9. I didn't go to the hospital.
10. Which apartment did you rent?
11. I heard it in the cafeteria.
12. The teacher gave us a lot of homework.

Page 40

Listen and circle the word you hear.

1. I'd like a three-bedroom apartment.
2. Is there anything available downtown?
3. We can't pay more than $560.
4. That includes everything except electricity.
5. Are pets allowed?
6. The neighborhood is very quiet.
7. I'd like a washer and dryer.
8. Are utilities included in the rent?
9. Is the apartment near a bus line?
10. I need an apartment within walking distance of the university.
11. The neighborhood is very convenient.
12. That includes everything except health club dues.

Page 41

Listen and choose the correct response.

1. Could you do me a favor?
2. Could you run over to the store? We need a few things.
3. What do you want me to get?
4. Could you pick up some milk?
5. How many bananas do we need?
6. How much cheese do you want me to get?
7. Is that everything?

8. How much tuna fish should I get?
9. What should we buy to drink?
10. Do we need any toothpaste?
11. How much mayonnaise do you want?
12. Do we have any ice cream in the refrigerator?

Page 44

Listen and choose the correct line to complete the conversation.

1. A. Cheese is in the Dairy Section, Aisle A.
   B. I'm sorry. Did you say Aisle A?
2. A. You can find bug spray in Household Supplies, Aisle G.
   B. Did you say Aisle G?
3. A. Excuse me. Where can I find apple cider?
   B. Look in the Produce Section, Aisle 5.
   A. I'm sorry. Did you say Aisle 9?
4. A. Taco shells are in the Imported Foods Section, Aisle C.
   B. Aisle C?
5. A. Where can I find toothpicks?
   B. They're in Aisle M.
   A. I'm sorry. Did you say Aisle N?
6. A. Lamb chops are with the Frozen Foods, Aisle 7.
   B. Aisle 7?

Page 46

Listen and circle the correct price.

1. That comes to $12.50.
2. The total is $10.54.
3. Your change is $2.40.
4. That'll be $6.76.
5. That comes to $12.25.
6. The total is $30.13.
7. That'll be $1.99.
8. Your change is $.90.
9. That comes to $3.80.
10. The total is $1.17.

Page 48

Do you remember the ingredients of the foods on student text page 68? Listen and write the number under the correct food.

1. A. This is delicious! What's in it?
   B. Let's see . . . a few eggs, a little flour, a little Italian cheese, and a little tomato sauce.
2. A. These are fantastic! What's in them?
   B. Let me see . . . a little pork, a little cabbage, and a few bean sprouts.
3. A. This is excellent! What's in it?
   B. Let me think . . . a little water, a few beets, a little sour cream, and a few onions.
4. A. This is wonderful! What's in it?
   B. Let me see . . . a few eggplants, a few mushrooms, a little ground beef, and a little tomato sauce.
5. A. These are superb! What's in them?
   B. Let me think . . . a little flour, a little cheese, a few tomatoes, and a little ground beef.

Page 53

Listen and circle the word you hear.

1. The employees wore their new uniforms yesterday.
2. I write reports in my present job.
3. I've already made seven sandwiches.
4. We've already spoken to our supervisor.
5. Have you met the new employee yet?
6. I eat in the new cafeteria every day.
7. She's already done her work.
8. Has the supervisor seen Michael's letter of resignation yet?
9. Did the clerks take inventory last week?

Page 55

These people are talking at a high school reunion. Listen and put a check next to the things they've done.

A. Hello, George.
B. Oh hi, Jennifer. It's great to see you.
A. Good to see you, too. Tell me, George, what have you done since we finished high school?
B. Well, I've done a lot of things. I've written several books, I've been a counselor at a Family Service Center, and I've traveled to many different countries.
A. That's wonderful. It sounds like you've done a lot of interesting things.
B. How about you, Jennifer? What have YOU done since we finished high school?
A. Well, I've been busy, too. I've studied the piano, I've given ballet lessons, and I've even sung with a rock band.
B. That sounds great, Jennifer.

Page 56

Listen and circle the word you hear.

1. Barbara has taken ballet lessons since 1993.
2. Have you ever flown an airplane?
3. You haven't gone to the bank yet.
4. My daughter hasn't ridden a horse since she was a teenager.
5. Robert has already written his letter of resignation.
6. Have you ever been to London?

Page 58

Which sentence do you hear?

1. A. Can you use the Internet?
   B. Yes, I can. I've been using the Internet since 1995.
2. A. Do you know how to bake?
   B. Yes, I do. I've been baking for years.
3. A. Is Carla busy?
   B. Yes. She's been feeding the animals all morning.
4. A. Is your son able to prepare salads and omelettes?
   B. Yes. He's been preparing them for more than five years.
5. A. Do your parents like Florida?
   B. They love it! They've been living there for a year.
6. A. Have I been talking on the telephone too long?
   B. Well, you've been talking for an hour.

Page 60

Listen to each person's work history, and put a check next to the correct information.

1. In my present job, I've been doing engine tune-ups. And while I haven't changed tires in my current job, I changed tires in the job I had before that.
2. In my present job, I've been selling furniture. And while I haven't sold refrigerators in my current position, I sold refrigerators in the job I had before that.
3. In my present job, I've been writing news stories. And while I haven't written obituaries in my current position, I wrote obituaries in the job I had before that.
4. In my present job, I've been taking inventory. And while I haven't driven the delivery van in my current position, I drove the delivery van in the job I had before that.

Page 61

Listen to the interviews. What did each job applicant do wrong?

1. A. Good afternoon, Mr. Smally. Please sit down.
   B. Thank you.
   A. I see you worked as an office manager for three years. Could you tell me about your responsibilities?
   B. I had a lot of responsibilities. They were very difficult, and I quit the job.
   A. What kinds of responsibilities did you have?
   B. You know, I can't remember them very well.
2. A. Good morning, Ms. Short. Your interview was scheduled for 10:15, and it's now 11:30.
   B. I know, but I slept late. I'm sorry I wasn't able to be here on time.
   A. Well, Ms. Short, punctuality is very important in this company.
   B. I promise I'll never be late again.

3. A. Good afternoon, Mr. Curtis. It's nice to meet you.
   B. Nice to meet you, too. I'd like you to meet my brother Albert and my cousin Marvin. They came with me for the interview.
   A. Oh, I see.
4. A. Please sit down, Ms. Jackson.
   B. Thank you. Excuse me, Mr. Moody, but do you by any chance have any gum? I can't find mine.
   A. I'm afraid I don't, Ms. Jackson. I never chew gum.

Page 63

Listen and choose the next line of the conversation.

1. My dishwasher has flooded the kitchen!
2. Grandpa has just fallen down the stairs, and he can't walk!
3. A fire has broken out in the building on the corner!
4. A robber has just crawled through a window of my apartment!
5. There's been a strange animal noise in the fireplace all morning!
6. I think Aunt Louise has just had a heart attack!

Page 65

Listen and choose the correct answer.

1. Decongestant spray is in Aisle E, on the middle shelf.
2. The dry skin lotion you're looking for is in Aisle B, near the pharmacy.
3. Medicine for a stomachache is in the middle of Aisle D, across from the decongestant spray.
4. Medicine for a backache is in Aisle A, on the first shelf.
5. Eyedrops? Let me see . . . They're in Aisle C, on the middle shelf.
6. Cough medicine is in Aisle A, on the third shelf, next to the pharmacy.
7. Headache tablets are located in Aisle C, on the first shelf, just before the eyedrops.
8. Hair spray is located in the back of the store, next to the pharmacy.

Page 67

Listen and choose the sentence to finish the conversation.

1. I've had a headache for several days.
2. Our dog Bozo has been nauseous since yesterday.
3. All the people in the office have itchy, watery eyes.
4. My husband has had a terrible toothache since last night.
5. My daughter has a bad earache.
6. My skin has been very dry all winter.
7. Our cat hasn't been able to move her leg since she jumped out of a tree last Sunday.
8. A man in my apartment building fell down the stairs and hasn't been able to move his shoulder for three days.
9. There's been a bad accident on the expressway!
10. The elderly woman in Apartment 4G has had a heart attack!

Page 70

Listen and choose the sentence that is closest in meaning.

1. You should join an organization that helps people "kick the habit."
2. I strongly recommend that you cut back on your responsibilities.
3. It's essential for you to change your eating habits.
4. It might be a good idea to find a hobby that you like.
5. You have to begin an exercise routine.
6. I strongly urge you to eat less salty food.

Page 71

Listen and circle the word you hear.

1. Why don't they try warm milk with honey?
2. They've been nauseous for three days.
3. They're supposed to take the medicine every four hours.
4. When is their appointment?
5. They'll start eating less salty food next week.
6. They've tried home remedies for minor illnesses.

Page 75

Listen and choose the best response.

1. Could you do me a favor?
2. I'm confident I'd be able to sell computers.
3. It's amazing how little you can buy these days for $10.00!
4. I don't want to make manicotti for dinner. Do you have any other ideas?
5. You're supposed to set the tables by 11:00 o'clock.
6. Do you think you'll be able to type the letters today?
7. So, the apartment has two bedrooms and is $850 a month?
8. Do you have any suggestions about my back problems?

Page 76

Listen and put a check next to the sentence you hear.

1. Dishwashers are on "9."
2. Returns are at the rear of the store.
3. Gloves are near the side entrance.
4. Women's shoes are in Aisle G.

Page 79

Listen and circle the product the customer wants to buy.

1. I'd like the one with a self-cleaning oven.
2. I want the one that's also a calculator.
3. I need the one with 16 megabytes of memory.
4. I'd like the one with the 25-inch screen and remote control.
5. I want the one that makes 8 cups and beeps when it's ready.
6. I'd like the one with an automatic ice maker.

Page 81

Listen and choose the best response.

1. I bought a new color TV last night.
2. This is my new bedroom set.
3. Look at these jeans.
4. I got a black purse for the dance next weekend.
5. I want to buy a new car.
6. My son needs a pair of new sneakers.
7. I'm going to buy a coffeemaker.
8. I really like this sweater.
9. We're interested in a gas range.
10. We're looking for a sofa.

Page 83

Listen and choose the best response.

1. I'd like to return these gloves. They're too dark.
2. This VCR is too difficult to operate.
3. Let's return this necktie. It's too conservative.
4. I don't want this sofa. It's too big.
5. That coffeemaker only makes 4 cups. It's too small.
6. This shortwave radio is too weak.
7. I want to exchange this coat for a shorter one.
8. The prices in this store are too high.

Page 84

Listen and choose the correct answer.

Conversation 1

A. I'd like to mail this package to Houston.
B. How would you like to send it?
A. First class, please.
B. Okay. It's seven pounds, so that's eleven dollars and sixty-nine cents.
A. Eleven sixty-nine?
B. Well, it could be sent parcel post, if you want. It would be eight dollars and seventy-five cents. It'll take about ten days.
A. Okay. I'll send it parcel post.

Conversation 2

A. I'd like to mail this package to Miami.

B. How would you like to send it?
A. First class, please.
B. Okay. It's twelve pounds, so that's ten dollars and thirty-one cents.
A. Ten thirty-one? Would it be cheaper to send it parcel post?
B. Oh, yes. Parcel post to Miami is five eighty-nine.
A. Will it take longer to get there?
B. Yes. It'll take about a week.
A. Hmm. It's a wedding present, and the wedding is this Saturday. I'd better send it first class.

Page 87

Listen and put a check next to what these people are going to do today.

1. A. What do you want to do today?
   B. How about seeing a movie?
   A. Hmm. I don't feel like seeing a movie. Any other ideas?
   B. How about going jogging?
   A. Good idea. We haven't gone jogging in a long time.
2. A. How about having a picnic today?
   B. I'm not really in the mood for a picnic. How about going bowling?
   A. Good idea! We haven't gone bowling in a long time.
3. A. What do you feel like doing today?
   B. I'm in the mood to play tennis.
   A. Hmm. I don't really want to play tennis. Any other suggestions?
   B. We could go to the ballgame.
   A. Good idea!
4. A. What about going swimming today?
   B. I'm not really in the mood to go swimming. How about going fishing?
   A. Good idea! We haven't gone fishing in a long time.

Page 89

Listen and circle what these people are going to do today.

1. Let's go for a walk in the mountains today!
2. I don't feel like playing tennis. I'd prefer to go bowling.
3. Let's go to an adventure movie!
4. Come on, Bobby! Let's play "hide and seek!"
5. Let's get together this weekend. I'd like to go to a museum.
6. How about packing a lunch and going to the lake?

Page 90

Listen and choose the best activity based on the weather.

1. It's going to be very cold and windy today.
2. The weather tomorrow will be warm and sunny.
3. It'll be rainy and warm tomorrow, with a chance of a little sunshine in the afternoon.
4. It's foggy today, so be careful driving!
5. There are several inches of snow predicted for the metropolitan area tomorrow.
6. It's 85 degrees today, and tomorrow will be even warmer!

Page 94

Listen and circle the word you hear.

1. Did you watch the weather forecast?
2. I got a letter from my cousin yesterday. She hadn't written in a long time.
3. My dog was hurt in an accident.
4. He didn't send any money in the package.
5. I said this car costs $15,000.
6. No, I hadn't gone to the beach the weekend before.
7. I hadn't seen her in ages.
8. Phillip has never flown before.
9. We went to the mountains last week. We hadn't hiked since last summer.
10. We had wanted to play golf, but the weather was bad.
11. Have you ever made sushi?
12. Why don't we skate at the lake?
13. Who drove you to the movie?
14. I wanted to go skiing last weekend, but I hadn't bought skis yet.
15. She had drawn some beautiful pictures.

Page 95

Listen and decide what these people are talking about.

1. A. The truth is, we didn't have a very good time. The water was choppy, and our cabins were very small.
   B. That's too bad. You had been looking forward to it for a long time.
2. A. Did you enjoy it?
   B. Not really. The food was terrible, and the service was slow.
   A. I'm sorry to hear that. You had been talking about going there for weeks!
3. A. How was it?
   B. It was awful! The ride was bumpy, and they showed a movie I had already seen.
4. A. Did you have a good time?
   B. Not really. The hotel was crowded, and the weather was miserable.
   A. That's a shame. You had been looking forward to it for a long time.
5. A. Did you have a good time?
   B. Not really. The band was too loud, and they played very old-fashioned music.
6. A. How was it?
   B. I didn't enjoy it very much. It was very boring, and we had terrible seats.
   A. That's too bad. You had really been looking forward to seeing it.

Page 97

Listen and choose the best name for the movie.

1. City Cinema is proud to present a new documentary about health problems. Showing daily at 8 and 10 P.M.
2. Thank you for calling the Mall Cinema. We have a new feature film. It's a comedy starring Gene Little and Sally Gold. Come and see it daily at 7 and 9 P.M.
3. Bring the kids to the East Town Mall Cinema to see a new computer-generated cartoon about two lovable animals. Showing every afternoon at 1 and 3 P.M.
4. The West Town Mall Cinema is featuring a new children's film starring everybody's favorite bears. Shows are daily at 2 and 4 P.M.
5. Join us for a foreign adventure at the Downtown Cinema every day at 5 and 7 P.M.
6. The Baker Theater is proud to present a new western starring Bill Blades and Emily Rose. Shows are at 7:30 and 9:45 daily.

Page 100

Listen and choose the correct answer.

1. If you buy a TV, you should . . . .
2. Where do you want to . . . ?
3. Can you help me . . . ?
4. How about . . . ?
5. I don't feel like . . . .
6. These gloves are too small. I'd like to . . . .
7. I'm not really in the mood to . . . .
8. Why don't we . . . ?
9. I'd rather . . . .
10. Would you by any chance be interested in . . . ?

CORRELATION

ExpressWays Student Text/Activity Workbook

Student Text Pages	Activity Workbook Pages
Exit 1	
2–7	1–3
8–9	4
10–11	5–6
12–13	7–8
14–17	9–12
Exit 2	
20–23	13–15
24–27	16–18
28–29	19–21
30–33	22–24
Exit 3	
36–37	25–26
38–39	27–28
40–43	29–30
44–47	31–33
48–51	34–36
Exit 4	
56–59	39–40
60–63	41–42
64–65	43–44
66–67	45–46
68–69	47–48
70–73	49–50
Exit 5	
76–77	51
78–79	52–53
80–81	54–55
82–83	56
84–85	57
86–87	58–59
88–89	60
90–91	61–62

Student Text Pages	Activity Workbook Pages
Exit 6	
94–95	63
96–97	64
98–99	65
100–101	66–67
102–103	68–69
104–105	70
106–109	71–72
110–111	73
Exit 7	
116–117	76–77
118–119	78–79
120–121	80–81
122–125	82–83
126–129	84–85
130–131	86
Exit 8	
134–135	87
136–137	88–89
138–139	90
140–141	91–92
142–143	93–94
144–145	95
146–147	96–97
148–151	98